# Who Next...?

## A guide to children's authors

## 3rd Edition

Edited by

## Viv Warren and Mary Yardley

LISU Re... for Info... ...ughborough ...iversity

WARREN, Viv and YARDLEY, Mary, Editors
*Who Next...? A guide to children's authors*
Loughborough: LISU 2007

First published 1999, 3rd edition 2007
ISBN 9781905499069

© LISU 2007

We are grateful to the following for permission to use reproductions from their original cover images as follows:

*Dawn Undercover* by Anna Dale
*Larklight* by Philip Reeve
both reproduced by permission of Bloomsbury

*Blobheads Go Boing!* by Paul Stewart & Chris Riddell
*Jane Blonde Spies Trouble* by Jill Marshall
*Ms Wiz Mayhem* by Terence Blacker
all reproduced by permission of Macmillan Children's Books

*Clarice Bean, Don't Look Now* by Lauren Child
reproduced by permission of David Higham Associates and Orchard Books

*Horrid Henry and the Football Fiend* by Francesca Simon, illustrated by Tony Ross
reproduced by permission of Orion Children's Books

*Does Anyone Ever Listen?* by Rosie Rushton
Cover illustration by Sue Hellard
First published by Piccadilly Press Ltd. in 2006

*Harry and the Dinosaurs Make a Christmas Wish* by Ian Whybrow and Adrian Reynolds
*Mungo and the Picture Book Pirates* by Timothy Knapman and Adam Stower
*My Secret Unicorn: Rising Star* by Linda Chapman
all reproduced by permission of Puffin Books

*The Boy in the Striped Pyjamas* by John Boyne, David Fickling Books
*Eragon* by Christopher Paolini, illustrated by John Jude Palencar,
    illustration from the cover of *Eragon* copyright © John Jude Palencar, Corgi Books
*Payback* by Andy McNab and Robert Rigby, Corgi Books
*The Runaway Train* by Benedict Blathwayt, Red Fox
*Starring Tracy Beaker* by Jacqueline Wilson, Doubleday
*Traction Man Is Here* by Mini Grey, Red Fox
*Wintersmith* by Terry Pratchett, Doubleday
all reprinted by permission of The Random House Group Ltd

Cover design by Paul Atkins, Media Services, Loughborough University

Inside pages designed and typeset by Mary Ashworth and Sharon Fletcher, LISU

Printed by W & G Baird Ltd, Greystone Press, Antrim, N Ireland, BT41 2RS

Published and distributed by LISU, Loughborough University, Loughborough, LE11 3TU
Tel +44 (0)1509 635680 · Fax +44 (0)1509 635699 · Email lisu@lboro.ac.uk
http://www.lboro.ac.uk/departments/dis/lisu

# Foreword

It's wonderful when children get hooked on books and discover the joys of reading. There's often one fictional character that seems like a child's special friend. They stay loyal to Angelina or Clarice Bean or Thomas the Tank Engine or Horrid Henry and don't want to read about anyone else. As they get older children sometimes get fixated on one author in particular. They will only read J.K.Rowling or Roald Dahl - or maybe even Jacqueline Wilson.

This brilliant guide is a boon to parents, teachers and librarians because it offers so many other suggested authors. It's clearly set out and fun to use, and there's a very useful section on genres and themes. It's the perfect answer to get children to broaden their reading habits and discover the huge and varied and fantastic world of children's literature.

This brand new edition of *Who Next...?* has been skillfully edited by Mary Yardley and Viv Warren. The first edition was jointly edited by Norah Irvin and Lesley Cooper. I met Lesley several times and found her delightful and supremely knowledgeable about children's books. I was very sad when she died so young. Her daughter Naomi is now my much-cherished publicist. She cheerfully manages to look after me and her two little boys, Sam and Jake. They are already little bookworms. As they get older I'm sure Naomi will find this book very useful. I hope you will too.

Jacqueline Wilson

# The Editors

*Viv Warren* and *Mary Yardley* are qualified librarians with many years experience of working with children and young people in schools, in schools library services and in public libraries. Mary got to know the previous editors of *'Who Next...?'* whilst working for Hertfordshire Library Service. When Norah Irvin, the editor of the last edition decided to pass on the editorship, Mary was asked to take it on. Mary and Viv became colleagues whilst working for East Sussex County Council, when Viv was Head of Library Services to Children and Young People and Mary, Head of Information Management.

Between them they have experience of:

- setting up and running school and college libraries
- formulating a variety of policies for library services in East Sussex
- advising schools on books and book provision
- advising parents and teachers on books and reading
- selecting stock for schools, schools library services and public libraries
- running courses for teachers and parents on choosing and using books
- organising events to encourage parents and children to enjoy books together
- giving book talks to all ages
- setting up and running reading groups for both children and adults

Viv is now retired but keeps in touch - she was recently Chair of Brighton & Hove's Early Years Development and Childcare Partnership and is on the governing board of several schools. She delivers occasional book-related courses and has acted as co-ordinator for Family Learning events. Mary is currently working for Somerset Library and Information Service in a job share where she is responsible for buying all stock - children's and adult.

# Contents

Acknowledgements     ii

Introduction     iii

How to Use this Guide     v

Author Lists for Ages
    5-7     1
    8-11     33
    12-14     91

Genre and Themes     134
    Adventure     134
    Animals     135
    Ballet, Computers     136
    Crime, Death, Detective mystery, Diaries     137
    Disability, Environment, Fairy/folk     138
    Family     139
    Fantasy     140
    Friends     142
    Ghost/supernatural     143
    Historical     144
    Horror, Humour     145
    Illness, Letters     147
    Magic, Mystery     148
    Mythology, Other cultures     149
    Other lands, Pony/horse, Romance, School     150
    Science fiction, Sea/boats     151
    Social issues     152
    Space, Sport, Stage, Thrillers     153
    Traditional, Transport, War     154

The Rise of the Graphic Novel     155

Current Children's Book Prizes     157

Exploring Further and Keeping up to Date     167

Index     172

# Acknowledgements

As always we owe a debt of gratitude to many people without whose help this guide could not have been compiled.

We are especially grateful to Norah Irvin, the previous editor, who has been supportive throughout and who has been generous in imparting her expertise and know-how to help us in getting this new edition together finally.

Others who deserve a special measure of thanks are Susan Heyes, of West Sussex School Library Service, Ceri Roberts and Wendy Cole of Rhondda-Cynon-Taf Library Services, Grace Ryan of Borders Bookshop, Brighton, and Joy Tollington of Somerset Library Service.

The ideas and imagination of many people who have contributed, help to give the book a wider scope and relevance and we would like to acknowledge how difficult it is to find time to help with projects like ours with all the pressures there are in the workplace. Therefore, many thanks to the following who made time to contribute:

| | |
|---|---|
| Angela Allen | Leicestershire Library Service |
| Eileen Armstrong | Cramlington High School, Northumberland |
| Sue Bowtell | The Forest School, Winnersh, Berkshire |
| Liz Broekmann & her team | Slough Library Service |
| Annie Everall & her team | Derbyshire Library Service |
| Mel Gibson | Senior Lecturer in Childhood Studies & Trainer & Historian – Comics & Visual Literacies Northumbria University |
| Patsy Heap | Birmingham Library Service |
| Karen Horsfield | Somerset Library Service |
| Angela McNally | Sutton Schools Library Service |
| Glenys Morris | Brighton and Hove Library Service |
| Judy Ottaway | Buckinghamshire Libraries & Heritage |
| Jennifer Parsons | East Sussex Schools Library Service |
| Robert Patching | Brighton and Hove Library Service |
| Greta Paterson | Medway Library Service |

Lesley Sim and West Sussex Public and Schools Library Service Teams

Also, Peters Bookselling Services, Birmingham and Askews Booksellers, Preston.

We are also grateful to our publishers LISU, at Loughborough University, and in particular to Mary Ashworth and Sharon Fletcher, who have guided us with unfailing patience through delays and set backs and help through every technical and organisational problem.

Finally, thank yous to family and friends who have lived with us throughout!

*Viv Warren*          *Mary Yardley*

# Introduction

*Who Next...? A guide to children's authors* is designed as a tool to help parents, teachers and librarians in schools and public libraries to guide children who have already enjoyed stories by one writer to find other authors they will enjoy reading.

The book lists 537 writers of children's fiction, and with each name suggests other authors who write in a similar way. The idea is that you look up one of your favourite children's authors, then try reading a book by one of the other authors listed underneath. By moving from one entry to another readers can expand the number of writers they enjoy. The same system has been used successfully in a similar guide to adult fiction; also published by LISU, *Who Else Writes Like...? A reader's guide to fiction authors* is now in its fifth edition.

The links that have been made between authors are of genre and theme, and also of styles of writing, or similar aspects of characterisation and settings. Of course no author writes exactly like another and readers will not agree with all the choices. Questioning *Who Next...?* may be one of the pleasures of using it, and a source for discussion and debate.

Most of the authors listed have written several books. We have tried to include books that are easily available, so you should be able to find the recommended titles in either a library or available from a bookshop. Whilst recognising their importance in encouraging the love of reading, it was decided to exclude picture books for younger readers as the aim is to focus on the story rather than illustration. However, one or two classic picture books have been included as it is considered that they are multi-layered and work on any level for any age range of reader. A short list of Graphic Novels has been included for the first time, as more novels are being produced in this format, and they have certainly contributed to encouraging many young people to read. Some graphic novels appear in the main body of the book. These are examples which show how graphic novels can help towards a continuum in moving on to other authors. These titles are indicated in the text by GN after the title.

Also, in this edition we have tried to point up some titles aimed at young people with lower than average reading ages. These are in the main text and are indicated by BS after the title. This means that they have been produced by the publisher Barrington Stoke who publish books, written by popular authors, for children who have dyslexia, or who are struggling or reluctant readers – further information can be found on their website, www.barringtonstoke.co.uk. There are many other publishers who produce some titles with the same aim but BS are specialists.

*Who Next...?* is arranged by three 'audience age groups': children aged 5-7, 8-11 and 12-14. Where an author writes for more than one age group, this is shown. We have not attempted to define age ranges exactly as this is limiting, and our aim is to encourage children to read as widely as possible. We ask users of *Who Next...?* to bear in mind the preferences, abilities and needs of individual children.

We have also included in the text a selection of titles for each author so that readers trying an author new to them have some idea of where to start.

At the end of *Who Next...?* are indexes of authors by theme and genre as well as a list of prize winners. There is also a section entitled Exploring Further which suggests a small number of books, magazines and websites to enable readers to research further and to keep up to date.

We very much hope that the book will help many readers to enjoy more children's books

*Viv Warren*   *Mary Yardley*

# How to Use this Guide

## Author Lists

We have arranged the lists of authors by age range then alphabetically by author surname.

So, to use *Who Next...?*, first select the appropriate age range, 5–7, 8–11 or 12–14. Then, in the alphabetical list, locate the author you want to match. There you will find the suggested alternative authors.

For example, a reader who is nine years old and who likes Anthony Masters books might also enjoy stories by Deborah Abela, Enid Blyton, Simon Chapman, Pete Johnson, Allan Frewin Jones, Nick Shadow, R L Stine, Robert Swindells or Robert Westall.

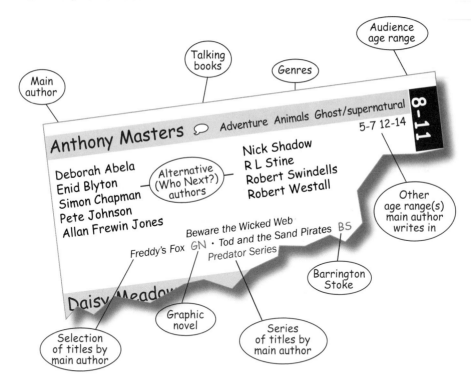

Where an author writes in a theme or genre, this is indicated. Do remember that some authors who frequently write in a particular category or for a specific age group sometimes produce a book in a quite different genre or for another age group. You can check this by reading the jacket details and summaries on the books themselves.

## Barrington Stoke

BS indicates that this title is published by Barrington Stoke who specialise in resources for dyslexic and struggling readers www.barringtonstoke.co.uk.

## Graphic Novels

A short list of Graphic Novels has been included for the first time (see pages 155-156), others are shown in the main text as GN after the title or series.

## Genres and Themes

If you only want a list of authors who write in a particular category or genre, such as Adventure or Animals, then turn straight to the Genre lists which start on page 134.

## Talking Books

Where books by a particular author are available on audio cassette or CD this is indicated by the symbol $\circlearrowright$

## Current Children's Book Prizes

Books which have been awarded a special prize are listed on pages 157-166.

We believe you will find this guide easy to use but please remember, it is not infallible. Finally, if you do need more information, ask - *library and bookshop staff are very willing to help.*

# Authors for Ages 5-7

## Anne Adeney
Animals Fairy/folk Humour

Andy Blackford
Anne Cassidy
Penny Dolan
Sue Graves
Dave Hanson

Maggie Moore
Margaret Nash
Jillian Powell
Hilary Robinson
Barrie Wade

*George and the Dragon · Hannibal's Noisy Day · I Can't Stand It!
Lighthouse Mouse · The Little Mermaid · The Pied Piper of Hamelin*

## Allan Ahlberg ⌒
Animals Family Humour

8-11

Jonathan Allen
Giles Andreae
Chris d'Lacey
P D Eastman
Vivian French

Kes Gray
Mini Grey
Anita Jeram
Theo Le Sieg
Dr Seuss

*Shopping Expedition
Fast Fox; Slow Dog · Funnybones Series · The Gaskitts*

## Jonathan Allen
Humour Magic

Allan Ahlberg
Terence Blacker
Humphrey Carpenter
Lauren Child

Jonathan Emmett
Ann Jungman
Jill Murphy
Shoo Rayner

*Wizard Grimweed Series*

## Scoular Anderson
Ghost/supernatural Historical
Humour Magic

Simon Bartram
Tony Bradman
Julia Jarman
Frank Rodgers
Dee Shulman

Wendy Smith
Paul Stewart
Karen Wallace
Jeanne Willis
Philip Wooderson

*Bubble Trouble · Mean Team From Mars
Rob the Roman Gets Eaten by a Lion (Nearly) · Scary Dog
Stan the Dog Series · Wizard's Boy Series*

# Giles Andreae 💬

8-11

Allan Ahlberg
Martyn Beardsley
Judy Brown
Julia Jarman

Timothy Knapman
Nick Sharratt
Ian Whybrow

*Billy Bonkers · Captain Flinn and the Pirate Dinosaurs*
*The Chimpanzees of Happytown · Giraffes Can't Dance · Princess Pearl*

# Laurence Anholt 💬

8-11

Adrian Boote
Herbie Brennan
Keith Brumpton
Lauren Child
Roald Dahl

Neil Gaiman
Mini Grey
Tony Mitton
Bob Wilson
Chris Wormell

*Seven for a Secret*
*The One and Only Series · Seriously Silly Rhymes · Seriously Silly Stories*

# Roy Apps 💬

8-11

Humphrey Carpenter
Jonathan Emmett
Alex Gutteridge

Ann Jungman
Kaye Umansky
Karen Wallace

*Stacey Stone Series · Twitches Series*

# Phyllis Arkle 💬

Henrietta Branford
Peter Clover
Jenny Dale

Tessa Krailing
Jill Tomlinson
Colin West

*The Railway Cat*
*The Railway Cat and the Horse · The Railway Cat's Secret*

# Antonia Barber

8-11

Ann Bryant
Harriet Castor

Adèle Geras

*Dancing Shoes Series*

> 💬 Some titles available as **Talking books**

## Simon Bartram
Diaries Fantasy

Scoular Anderson
Raymond Briggs
Emily Gravett

Mini Grey
Timothy Knapman

*Dougal's Deep Sea Diary · Man on the Moon*

## Martyn Beardsley
Adventure Humour

8-11

Giles Andreae
Tony Bradman
Alex Gutteridge

Tony Mitton
Karen Wallace

*Sir Gadabout Series*

## Stan and Jan Berenstain
Humour

P D Eastman
Anita Jeram
Theo Le Sieg

Hilary Robinson
Dr Seuss
Colin West

*Berenstain Bears on the Moon*
*Berenstain Bears on Wheels · C is for Clown*

## Terence Blacker
Humour Magic School

8-11 12-14

Jonathan Allen
Humphrey Carpenter
Lauren Child
Maeve Friel
Ann Jungman

Daisy Meadows
Jill Murphy
Ghillian Potts
Wendy Smith

*Ms Wiz Series*

## Andy Blackford
Humour

Anne Adeney
Anne Cassidy
John Cunliffe
Penny Dolan
Anita Jeram

James Marshall
Maggie Moore
Margaret Nash
Hilary Robinson
Barrie Wade

*Little Joe's Big Race*

Go to the back for lists of:
Authors by Genre · Graphic novels · Prize winners · Exploring further

## Malorie Blackman 💬

Adventure  Magic
Other lands  Science fiction
8-11 12-14

Lisa Bruce
Ann Cameron
Jamila Gavin

Julia Jarman
Hilda Offen
Jacqueline Wilson

*The Amazing Adventures of Girl Wonder*
*Ellie and the Cat · Sinclair Wonder Bear*

## Jon Blake 💬

Adventure  Family  Humour

Dennis Hamley
Sam McBratney

Colin McNaughton
Dyan Sheldon

*Dogsbottom School Series · House of Fun Series*

## Benedict Blathwayt 💬

Adventure  Transport

John Cunliffe

Kes Gray

*The Adventures of the Little Red Train Series*

## Adrian Boote

Adventure  Fantasy  Humour

Laurence Anholt
Keith Brumpton
Damon Burnard
Roald Dahl

Jonathan Emmett
Tony Mitton
Jeremy Strong

*The Ice Cream Cowboys · The Lemonade Genie*
*The Lollipop Knight · The Strawberry Sorcerer*

## Tony Bradman 💬

Fairy/folk  Fantasy
Ghost/supernatural  Humour
8-11

Scoular Anderson
Martyn Beardsley
Damon Burnard
Chris d'Lacey
Roald Dahl

John Grant
Tessa Krailing
Marilyn McLaughlin
Margaret Nash
Selina Young

*The Big Race · Dilly and the Goody-Goody · The Mummy Family Finds Fame*
*Creepy Crawlies Series · Happy Ever After Series*

## Henrietta Branford 💬

Adventure  Animals  Fantasy
8-11

Phyllis Arkle
Peter Clover

Pippa Goodhart
Jill Tomlinson

*Dimanche Diller at Sea · Dimanche Diller in Danger*
*Royal Blunder · Royal Blunder and the Haunted House*

## Herbie Brennan
Adventure Detective mysteries Humour

8-11

Laurence Anholt
Keith Brumpton

Roald Dahl
Jeremy Strong

*Eddie and the Bad Egg · Eddie the Duck*
*Franken Stella and the Video Shop Monster*

## Raymond Briggs
Humour

8-11

Simon Bartram
John Grant
Emily Gravett

Colin McNaughton
Dav Pilkey
Nick Sharratt

*The Bear · Father Christmas*
*Fungus the Bogeyman · The Snowman · Ug*

## Joyce Lankester Brisley 💬
Family Humour

Dorothy Edwards
Bel Mooney

Magdalen Nabb
Jenny Oldfield

*Milly Molly Mandy Stories*

## Jeff Brown 💬
Adventure Fantasy

Sally Gardner
John Grant
Sam McBratney
Megan McDonald

Dav Pilkey
Alf Prøysen
Jeremy Strong

*Flat Stanley Series*

## Judy Brown
Adventure Fantasy

Giles Andreae
Vivian French

Colin McNaughton
Ian Whybrow

*Pirate Princess Series*

## Marc Brown 💬
Animals Family Friends Humour

Damon Burnard
John Grant
Shirley Hughes
James Marshall

Frank Rodgers
Dr Seuss
Francesca Simon
Ian Whybrow

*Arthur Series*

## Lisa Bruce — Adventure  Friends  Other cultures

Malorie Blackman
Ann Cameron
Jamila Gavin
Mary Hoffman

Geraldine McCaughrean
Hilda Offen
Karen Wallace

*Jazeera in the Sun* · *Jazeera's Journey*
*Nani's Holiday* · *Rama's Return* · *Trouble for Deela*

## Keith Brumpton 〇 — Fantasy  Historical  Humour

Laurence Anholt
Adrian Boote
Herbie Brennan
Roald Dahl
Sam McBratney

Dav Pilkey
Gwyneth Rees
Jeremy Strong
Martin Waddell
Philip Wooderson

*Chariots on Fire!* · *Gruesome Twosome*
*Superheroes Down the Plughole* · *The Sword in the Scone*
*Kung Fu Pigs Series*

## Ann Bryant — Ballet  Friends

Antonia Barber
Harriet Castor

Adèle Geras

8-11

*The Great Swimming Race*
*Ballerina Dream Series*

## Janet Burchett and Sara Vogler — Humour  Sport

Rob Childs
Michael Coleman

Martin Waddell
Bob Wilson

*Little Terrors Series* · *The Tigers Series*

## Damon Burnard — Adventure  Humour

Adrian Boote
Tony Bradman
Marc Brown
Vivian French

Rose Impey
Paul Stewart
Ian Whybrow

*Bullysaurus Series* · *Frankly Frank Series* · *Little Bugs Series*

## Nick Butterworth — Animals Humour

John Cunliffe
Joyce Dunbar

Jan Fearnley
Beatrix Potter

*Percy's Park Series*

## Ann Cameron — Family Friends Humour Other cultures

Malorie Blackman
Lisa Bruce
Dorothy Edwards
Jamila Gavin

Shirley Hughes
Julia Jarman
Francesca Simon
Emily Smith

*Julian Series*

## Humphrey Carpenter — Humour Magic School

Jonathan Allen
Roy Apps
Terence Blacker
Maeve Friel
Peter Kavanagh

Daisy Meadows
Jill Murphy
Ghillian Potts
Kaye Umansky

*Mr Majeika Series*

## Anne Cassidy — Animals Fairy/folk Humour

12-14

Anne Adeney
Andy Blackford
Penny Dolan
Sue Graves
Dave Hanson

Maggie Moore
Margaret Nash
Jillian Powell
Hilary Robinson
Barrie Wade

*The Best Den Ever · Jasper and Jess · Jumping Josie · Puss in Boots*

## Harriet Castor — Animals Ballet Friends

Antonia Barber
Ann Bryant

Adèle Geras
Shoo Rayner

*Ballet Magic · Ballet Magic on Stage · The Dinosaurs Next Door*
*Fat Puss Series*

*Go to the back for lists of:*
Authors by Genre · Graphic novels · Prize winners · Exploring further

## Linda Chapman
Fantasy Magic Pony/horse

Maeve Friel
Diana Kimpton
Dick King-Smith
Elizabeth Lindsay
Kelly McKain

Daisy Meadows
Jenny Oldfield
Gwyneth Rees
Anna Wilson

8-11

*My Secret Unicorn Series · Not Quite a Mermaid Series*

## Lauren Child 💬
Fairy/folk Family Humour

Jonathan Allen
Laurence Anholt
Terence Blacker
Neil Gaiman
Emily Gravett

Kes Gray
Mini Grey
Alan Rusbridger
Kaye Umansky

8-11

*Beware of the Story Book Wolves · Hubert Horatio Bartle Bobton-Trent*
*The Princess and the Pea · Who's Afraid of the Big Bad Book?*
*Charlie and Lola Series*

## Rob Childs 💬
School Sport

Janet Burchett and Sara Vogler
Michael Coleman

Anthony Masters
Martin Waddell

8-11

*The Big Drop · Keepers Ball · Strike*

## Emma Chichester Clark
Animals Friends Humour

Joyce Dunbar
Rose Impey
Arnold Lobel

James Marshall
Jill Tomlinson

*Melrose and Croc Series*

## Peter Clover
Adventure Animals Pony/horse

Phyllis Arkle
Henrietta Branford
Jenny Dale
Lucy Daniels

Diana Kimpton
Dick King-Smith
Elizabeth Lindsay
Jill Tomlinson

*Donkey Diaries · Sheltie Series*

8

## Michael Coleman
**Friends Humour School Sport**
8-11

Janet Burchett and Sara Vogler
Rob Childs

Martin Waddell
Bob Wilson

*Fizzy in the Spotlight*
*Angels FC Series*

## Andrew Cope
**Adventure Animals Humour**
8-11

Jonathan Emmett
Hiawyn Oram

Colin West

*Spy Dog · Spy Dog 2*

## June Crebbin
**Fantasy Ghost/supernatural Humour**

Roald Dahl
Alan Durant
Jan Fearnley

Anne Fine
Vivian French

*Dragon Test · Hal the Pirate*
*Lucy and the Firestone · The King's Shopping*

## John Cunliffe ⌒
**Friends Humour**

Andy Blackford
Benedict Blathwayt
Nick Butterworth

Sally Grindley
Jillian Powell

*Postman Pat Series*

## Chris d'Lacey
**Animals Family Humour**
8-11

Allan Ahlberg
Tony Bradman
Pippa Goodhart
Geraldine McCaughrean

Bel Mooney
Michael Morpurgo
Selina Young

*Dexter's Journey · Juggling with Jeremy · Lofty*

## Roald Dahl ⌒
**Fantasy Humour**
8-11

Laurence Anholt
Adrian Boote
Tony Bradman
Herbie Brennan
Keith Brumpton

June Crebbin
Sam McBratney
Francesca Simon
Jeremy Strong
Bob Wilson

*Fantastic Mr Fox · The Magic Finger · The Twits*

# Jenny Dale

Animals

| | | 8-11 |
|---|---|---|
| Phyllis Arkle | Dick King-Smith | |
| Peter Clover | Tessa Krailing | |
| Lucy Daniels | Hiawyn Oram | |
| Adèle Geras | Jill Tomlinson | |
| Diana Kimpton | | |

*Best Friends Series · Kitten Tales Series*
*Pony Tales Series · Puppy Tales Series*

# Lucy Daniels

Animals  Friends

| | | 8-11 |
|---|---|---|
| Peter Clover | Dick King-Smith | |
| Jenny Dale | Tessa Krailing | |
| Kathy Henderson | Elizabeth Lindsay | |
| Diana Kimpton | | |

*Animal Ark Pets Series · Little Animal Ark Series*

# Penny Dolan

Animals  Ghost/supernatural  Humour

| | |
|---|---|
| Anne Adeney | Maggie Moore |
| Andy Blackford | Margaret Nash |
| Anne Cassidy | Jillian Powell |
| Sue Graves | Hilary Robinson |
| Karina Law | Barrie Wade |

*The Apple Tree Alien · The Little Red Hen · Moo!*
*Ghostly Tales*

# Julia Donaldson

Animals  Fantasy

| | |
|---|---|
| Joyce Dunbar | Michael Morpurgo |
| Jan Fearnley | Chris Riddell |
| Kes Gray | Chris Wormell |
| Timothy Knapman | |

*Charlie Cook's Favourite Book*
*The Gruffalo · The Gruffalo's Child · The Quick Brown Fox Cub*
*The Smartest Giant in Town · The Snail and the Whale*
*Princess Mirror-Belle Series*

> ⟨ Some titles available as **Talking books** ⟩

## Malachy Doyle

Fairy/folk Historical Humour

Dennis Hamley
Rose Impey

Geraldine McCaughrean

8-11

*Antonio on the Other Side of the World, Getting Smaller*
*The Great Hunger* · *The Ugly Great Giant* · *When a Zeeder Met a Xyder*

## Joyce Dunbar

Animals Friends Humour

Nick Butterworth
Emma Chichester Clark
Julia Donaldson
Jan Fearnley
Vivian French

Arnold Lobel
James Marshall
Michael Morpurgo
Beatrix Potter
Alison Uttley

*Magic Lemonade* · *The Railway Angel*
*Mouse and Mole Series*

## Helen Dunmore 💬

Family Friends War 1939-45

Anne Fine
Jamila Gavin

Bel Mooney

8-11

*Allie Away* · *Amina's Blanket* · *Tara's Tree House*

## Alan Durant 💬

Humour

June Crebbin
Oliver Jeffers

Shoo Rayner
Paul Stewart

8-11

*Burger Boy* · *Brown Bear Gets in Shape* · *Flying South*
*Happy Birthday Spider McDrew* · *That's Not Right!*

## P D Eastman

Humour

Allan Ahlberg
Stan and Jan Berenstain

Theo Le Sieg
Dr Seuss

*Are You My Mother?* · *Go Dog Go* · *Sam and the Firefly*

---

Go to the back for
lists of:
Authors by Genre
Graphic novels
Prize winners
Further reading

## Dorothy Edwards 💬 — Family Friends Humour

Joyce Lankester Brisley
Ann Cameron
Jamila Gavin
Mary Hoffman

Shirley Hughes
Bel Mooney
Magdalen Nabb

*My Naughty Little Sister* • *My Naughty Little Sister and Bad Harry*
*More My Naughty Little Sister Stories*

## Jonathan Emmett — Adventure Friends Humour Magic

Jonathan Allen
Roy Apps
Adrian Boote

Andrew Cope
Damian Harvey
Ann Jungman

*Bringing Down the Moon* • *Someone Bigger* • *What Friends Do Best*
*Conjuror's Cookbook Series*

## Jan Fearnley 💬 — Humour

Nick Butterworth
June Crebbin
Julia Donaldson

Joyce Dunbar
Frank Rodgers

*Colin and the Curly Claw* • *Mabel and Max* • *A Very Proper Fox*

## Anne Fine 💬 — Family Fantasy Friends Ghost/supernatural

June Crebbin
Helen Dunmore
Adèle Geras
Joan Lingard

Hilary McKay
Michael Morpurgo
Jacqueline Wilson

8-11 12-14

*The Diary of a Killer Cat* • *Jamie and Angus Stories*
*Nag Club* • *Return of the Killer Cat*

## Vivian French 💬 — Animals Humour

Allan Ahlberg
Judy Brown
Damon Burnard
June Crebbin
Joyce Dunbar

Sally Grindley
Diana Kimpton
Daisy Meadows
Anna Wilson
Selina Young

*Brian the Giant* • *The Cat in the Coat* • *Cave-Baby and the Mammoth*
*I Wish I Was an Alien* • *Pig in Love* • *Sharp Sheep*
*Iggy Pig Series* • *Space Dog Series* • *The Tiara Club Series*

## Maeve Friel 💬

Magic

8-11

Terence Blacker
Humphrey Carpenter
Linda Chapman
Alex Gutteridge
Kelly McKain

Daisy Meadows
Jill Murphy
Ghillian Potts
Wendy Smith

*Witch in Training Series*

## Neil Gaiman

Animals Family Fantasy

8-11

Laurence Anholt
Lauren Child
Mini Grey

Oliver Jeffers
Colin McNaughton

*The Day I Swapped My Dad for Two Goldfish*
*The Wolves in the Walls*

## Sally Gardner 💬

Fantasy

8-11 12-14

Jeff Brown

Hilda Offen

*Magical Children Series*

## Jamila Gavin

Family Friends Mythology Other cultures

8-11 12-14

Malorie Blackman
Lisa Bruce
Ann Cameron
Helen Dunmore

Dorothy Edwards
Julia Jarman
Margaret Mayo

*Deadly Friend • Fine Feathered Friend*

## Adèle Geras 💬

Animals Ballet Family

8-11 12-14

Antonia Barber
Ann Bryant
Harriet Castor
Jenny Dale

Anne Fine
Kathy Henderson
Tessa Krailing

*Good Luck Louisa • Louisa the Ballerina*
*Cats of Cuckoo Square Series*

💬 Some titles available as Talking books

## Pippa Goodhart
Animals Fantasy

Henrietta Branford
Chris d'Lacey
Mary Hoffman

Michael Morpurgo
Jill Tomlinson

8-11

*Dragon Boy · Friends Forever*
*Hoppy Birthday Jo-Jo · Ronnie's Treasure Hunt*
*Maxine and Minnie Series*

## John Grant
Adventure Historical

Tony Bradman
Raymond Briggs
Jeff Brown

Marc Brown
Nick Sharratt

*Littlenose Series*

## Sue Graves
Humour

Anne Adeney
Anne Cassidy
Penny Dolan

Dave Hanson
Maggie Moore
Margaret Nash

*A Busy Week · The Great Escape*
*Miss Muffet and the Spider · Oh George! · Percy the Postman*

## Emily Gravett
Humour

Simon Bartram
Raymond Briggs
Lauren Child
Mini Grey

Oliver Jeffers
Timothy Knapman
Chris Wormell

*Wolves*

## Kes Gray ○
Animals Family Humour

Allan Ahlberg
Benedict Blathwayt
Lauren Child

Julia Donaldson
Nick Sharratt
Kaye Umansky

8-11

*Cluck O'Clock · Eat Your Peas · Vesuvius Poovius*
*Nelly the Monster Sitter Series · Daisy Stories*

Go to the back for lists of:
Authors by Genre · Graphic novels · Prize winners · Exploring further

## Mini Grey

Fairy/folk Fantasy Humour

Allan Ahlberg
Laurence Anholt
Simon Bartram
Lauren Child
Neil Gaiman

Emily Gravett
Timothy Knapman
Hiawyn Oram
Chris Wormell

*The Adventures of the Dish and the Spoon*
*The Pea and the Princess* · *Traction Man is Here*

## Sally Grindley ⌒

Adventure Animals Friends

8-11

John Cunliffe
Vivian French
Barbara Mitchelhill

Nicola Moon
Margaret Ryan

*The Big What Are Friends For Storybook*
*Captain Pepper's Pets* · *The Giant Postman* · *Mulberry Goes to School*

## Alex Gutteridge ⌒

Adventure Humour Magic

Roy Apps
Martyn Beardsley
Maeve Friel
Ann Jungman
Peter Kavanagh

Diana Kimpton
Timothy Knapman
Colin McNaughton
Jill Murphy
Margaret Ryan

*Pirate Polly Rules the Waves*
*Princess Posy, Knight-in-Training* · *Witch Wendy Works Her Magic*

## Dennis Hamley

Historical War 1939-45

8-11

Jon Blake
Malachy Doyle

Karen Wallace

*D-Day!* · *Tunnel Rescue*

## Dave Hanson

Humour

Anne Adeney
Anne Cassidy
Sue Graves
Maggie Moore

Margaret Nash
Jillian Powell
Hilary Robinson
Barrie Wade

*We're Going Camping* · *What Now Puss?*

## Damian Harvey

Humour

Jonathan Emmett                    Jeanne Willis
Ian Whybrow

*A Band of Dirty Pirates · Big Bad Bart · Captain Cool*
*Cockerel's Big Egg · Monster Cake · Oggy and the Dinosaur*
*Tales of Robin Hood*

## Kathy Henderson

Animals  Environment  Family

Lucy Daniels                      Dick King-Smith
Adèle Geras                       Michael Morpurgo
Diana Kimpton

*And the Good Brown Earth · Dog Story · Fearless Fitzroy*

## Mary Hoffman

Adventure  Animals  Fantasy  Humour

Lisa Bruce                        Pippa Goodhart        12-14
Dorothy Edwards                   Hiawyn Oram

*Bravo, Grace! · The Colour of Home · Dracula's Daughter*

## Mary Hooper ⌒

Adventure  Family  Historical  Humour

Julia Jarman                      Daniel Postgate       8-11 12-14
Hilary McKay                      Karen Wallace

*The Great Twin Trick · Spook Spotting*
*Mischief and Mayhem · Spooks and Scares*

## Shirley Hughes

Family  Humour

Marc Brown                        Dorothy Edwards
Ann Cameron                       Ian Whybrow

*Dogger*
*Alfie Stories · Ollie and Me Series*

> Go to the back for
> lists of:
> Authors by Genre
> Graphic novels
> Prize winners
> Further reading

16

## Rose Impey 💬     Animals Family Humour Traditional

8-11

Damon Burnard
Emma Chichester Clark
Malachy Doyle
Karina Law
Arnold Lobel

James Marshall
Tony Mitton
Hiawyn Oram
Alan Rusbridger
Margaret Ryan

*Monster and Frog and the Magic Show*
*Monster and Frog and the Slippery Wallpaper*
*Animal Crackers Series* · *Scout and Ace Series*
*Titchy Witch Series* · *Twice Upon a Time Series*

## Julia Jarman 💬     Adventure Animals Humour Magic

8-11

Scoular Anderson
Giles Andreae
Malorie Blackman
Ann Cameron
Jamila Gavin

Mary Hooper
Beatrix Potter
Chris Powling
Alan Rusbridger
Dee Shulman

*Flying Friends* · *The Jessame Stories* · *The Magic Backpack*
*Tales from Whispery Wood*

## Oliver Jeffers 💬     Fantasy Friends Humour

Alan Durant
Neil Gaiman

Emily Gravett
Chris Wormell

*The Incredible Book Eating Boy* · *Lost and Found*

## Anita Jeram     Animals Humour

Allan Ahlberg
Stan and Jan Berenstain
Andy Blackford

Jillian Powell
Colin West

*Daisy Dare* · *The Most Obedient Dog in the World*
*Contrary Mary Series*

## Ann Jungman 💬     Adventure Fantasy Humour Magic

Jonathan Allen
Roy Apps
Terence Blacker
Jonathan Emmett

Alex Gutteridge
Jill Murphy
Margaret Ryan

*Bold Bad Ben and the Beastly Bandit* · *Dragon Disasters*
*Septimouse, Big Cheese* · *School for Dragons*
*Broomstick Series* · *Frank N Stein Series*

17

## Peter Kavanagh · Adventure Magic

Humphrey Carpenter
Alex Gutteridge

Francesca Simon

*Arthur the Outlaw · Arthur the Wizard*

## Diana Kimpton · Adventure Pony/horse

Linda Chapman
Peter Clover
Jenny Dale
Lucy Daniels
Vivian French

Alex Gutteridge
Kathy Henderson
Tessa Krailing
Elizabeth Lindsay

*The Pony Mad Princess Series*

## Dick King-Smith 💬 · Animals Family Fantasy Humour

8-11

Linda Chapman
Peter Clover
Jenny Dale
Lucy Daniels
Kathy Henderson

Bel Mooney
Michael Morpurgo
Magdalen Nabb
Tony and Jan Payne
Jill Tomlinson

*The Adventurous Snail · All Because of Jackson · Aristotle*
*The Catlady · Dinosaur Trouble · Hairy Hezekiah*
*The Sophie Stories*

## Timothy Knapman · Adventure Fantasy

Giles Andreae
Simon Bartram
Julia Donaldson
Emily Gravett
Mini Grey

Alex Gutteridge
Colin McNaughton
Nick Sharratt
Ian Whybrow

*Mungo and the Picturebook Pirates*

## Tessa Krailing · Animals Friends

Phyllis Arkle
Tony Bradman
Jenny Dale

Lucy Daniels
Adèle Geras
Diana Kimpton

*Petsitters Club Series · Lizzie Longbody Series*

## Karina Law

5-7

Fairy/folk  Family  Humour

Penny Dolan
Rose Impey
Maggie Moore

Margaret Nash
Jillian Powell

*Marlowe's Mum and the Tree House*
*The Truth About Hansel and Gretel* · *The Truth About Those Billy Goats*

## Theo Le Sieg

Humour

Allan Ahlberg
Stan and Jan Berenstain

P D Eastman
Dr Seuss

*I Wish That I Had Duck Feet*
*Please Try to Remember the First of Octember* · *Wacky Wednesday*

## Elizabeth Lindsay

Adventure  Animals  Magic  Pony/horse

8-11

Linda Chapman
Peter Clover
Lucy Daniels

Diana Kimpton
Daisy Meadows
Jenny Oldfield

*Magic Pony Series*

## Joan Lingard ⌒

Animals  Family

12-14

Anne Fine

Jenny Nimmo

*Tom and the Tree House*
*Tilly and the Badgers* · *Tilly and the Wild Goats*

## Arnold Lobel ⌒

Animals  Humour

Emma Chichester Clark
Joyce Dunbar
Rose Impey
James Marshall

Nicola Moon
Beatrix Potter
Selina Young

*Days with Frog and Toad* · *Mouse Tales* · *Owl at Home*

⌒ Some titles available as Talking books

# Sam McBratney  Adventure Humour School Science fiction

Jon Blake
Jeff Brown
Keith Brumpton
Roald Dahl

Colin McNaughton
Ghillian Potts
Dyan Sheldon

*Art You're Magic · Kristel Dimond, Timecop*
*Stranger From Somewhere in Time*
*Jimmy Zest Series*

# Geraldine McCaughrean  Animals Humour Mythology

Lisa Bruce
Chris d'Lacey
Malachy Doyle

Margaret Mayo
Saviour Pirotta

8-11 12-14

*Jalopy · Noah and Nelly*
*Zeus Conquers the Titans*

# Megan McDonald

Fantasy Humour

Jeff Brown

Lauren Child

8-11

*Stink: the Incredible Shrinking Kid*
*Stink and the Incredible Supergalactic Jawbreaker*

# Kelly McKain

Fantasy Magic

Linda Chapman
Maeve Friel
Daisy Meadows

Barbara Mitchelhill
Gwyneth Rees
Anna Wilson

8-11

*Mermaid Rock Series*

# Hilary McKay

Family Friends

Anne Fine
Mary Hooper

Jacqueline Wilson

8-11 12-14

*Beetle and Friends Series*
*Paradise House Series · Pudding Bag School Series*

---

Go to the back for lists of:
Authors by Genre · Graphic novels · Prize winners · Exploring further

## Marilyn McLaughlin

5-7

Adventure  Friends  Humour

Tony Bradman
Magdalen Nabb
Jenny Oldfield

Dyan Sheldon
Francesca Simon

*Fierce Milly Series*

## Colin McNaughton

Adventure  Humour

Jon Blake
Raymond Briggs
Judy Brown
Neil Gaiman
Alex Gutteridge
Timothy Knapman

Sam McBratney
Dav Pilkey
Chris Riddell
Margaret Ryan
Dr Seuss

*Captain Abdul's Little Treasure · Captain Abdul's Pirate School*
*Jolly Roger and the Pirates of Abdul the Skinhead*

## James Marshall

Animals  Humour

Andy Blackford
Marc Brown
Emma Chichester Clark
Joyce Dunbar

Rose Impey
Arnold Lobel
Shoo Rayner

*Fox on Stage · Fox Outfoxed*

## Anthony Masters

Animals  Ghost/supernatural
Historical  Humour
8-11 12-14

Rob Childs
Barbara Mitchelhill

Nicola Moon
Karen Wallace

*Doughnut Danger · Ricky's Rat Gang*

## Margaret Mayo

Mythology

Jamila Gavin
Geraldine McCaughrean

Saviour Pirotta

*Creation Myths Series · First Fairy Tales Series*
*Magical Tales From Around the World Series*

💬 Some titles available as Talking books

## Daisy Meadows 💬      Magic

8-11

Terence Blacker      Elizabeth Lindsay
Humphrey Carpenter      Kelly McKain
Linda Chapman      Gwyneth Rees
Vivian French      Margaret Ryan
Maeve Friel      Anna Wilson

*The Jewel Fairies* · *The Party Fairies*
*The Pet Keeper Fairies* · *The Weather Fairies*

## Barbara Mitchelhill     Family Ghost/supernatural Humour

8-11

Sally Grindley      Kelly McKain
Anthony Masters

*Amy's Dragon* · *Amy's Mermaid*
*Eric Series*

## Tony Mitton      Humour Mythology

Laurence Anholt      Rose Impey
Martyn Beardsley      Alan Rusbridger
Adrian Boote      Kaye Umansky

*Crazy Camelot Capers Series* · *Happy Ever After Series* · *Raps Series*

## Nicola Moon      Animals Family Humour

Sally Grindley      Anthony Masters
Arnold Lobel      Jillian Powell

*Alligator Tails and Crocodile Cakes* · *J J Rabbit and the Monster*
*Margarine and Marbles* · *Noisy Neighbours*

## Bel Mooney 💬      Family Humour

Joyce Lankester Brisley      Magdalen Nabb
Chris d'Lacey      Jenny Oldfield
Helen Dunmore      Tony and Jan Payne
Dorothy Edwards      Francesca Simon
Dick King-Smith      Jacqueline Wilson

*Mr Tubbs is Lost* · *Who Loves Mr Tubbs*
*Kitty and Friends Series*

## Maggie Moore
Fairy/folk Humour

Anne Adeney
Andy Blackford
Anne Cassidy
Penny Dolan

Sue Graves
Dave Hanson
Karina Law
Barrie Wade

*Jack and the Beanstalk · Little Red Riding Hood
The Three Little Pigs · The Ugly Duckling*

## Michael Morpurgo
Animals Fairy/folk Family

8-11 12-14

Chris d'Lacey
Julia Donaldson
Joyce Dunbar
Anne Fine

Pippa Goodhart
Kathy Henderson
Dick King-Smith

*Cockadoodle-Doo, Mr Sultana!
Cool as a Cucumber · Dolphin Boy · Skip*

## Jill Murphy ⌒
Humour Magic

8-11

Jonathan Allen
Terence Blacker
Humphrey Carpenter
Maeve Friel

Alex Gutteridge
Ann Jungman
Ghillian Potts

*The Worst Witch Series*

## Magdalen Nabb
Family Friends

Joyce Lankester Brisley
Dorothy Edwards
Dick King-Smith
Marilyn McLaughlin

Bel Mooney
Jenny Oldfield
Tony and Jan Payne

*Josie Smith Series*

## Margaret Nash
Fairy/folk Humour

Anne Adeney
Andy Blackford
Tony Bradman
Anne Cassidy
Penny Dolan

Sue Graves
Dave Hanson
Karina Law
Jillian Powell
Hilary Robinson

*Dick Whittington · The North Wind and the Sun
Sleeping Beauty · Thumbelina*

# Jenny Nimmo 💬
Animals  Family  Fantasy  Magic

Joan Lingard
Angie Sage

Colin West

8-11

*Delilah and the Dishwasher Dogs*
*Invisible Vinnie · Matty Mouse · The Stone Mouse*

## Hilda Offen
Adventure  Family

Malorie Blackman
Lisa Bruce
Sally Gardner

Hiawyn Oram
Daniel Postgate

*Rita the Rescuer Series*

## Jenny Oldfield
Friends  Humour  Magic  School

Joyce Lankester Brisley
Linda Chapman
Elizabeth Lindsay
Marilyn McLaughlin

Bel Mooney
Magdalen Nabb
Francesca Simon

8-11

*Definitely Daisy Series · My Magical Pony Series*

## Hiawyn Oram
Adventure  Animals  Humour  Magic

Andrew Cope
Jenny Dale
Mini Grey
Mary Hoffman

Rose Impey
Hilda Offen
Gwyneth Rees
Alan Rusbridger

*The Big Brown Bap Master · The Wrong Overcoat*
*Animal Heroes Series · Beetle and Bugs Series*
*Forever Street Fairies Series · Mona the Vampire Series*

## Tony and Jan Payne 💬
Family  Humour

Dick King-Smith
Bel Mooney

Magdalen Nabb
Francesca Simon

*Hippo-not-amus*
*Annie Stories*

💬 Some titles available as **Talking books**

## Dav Pilkey

Raymond Briggs
Jeff Brown
Keith Brumpton

Colin McNaughton
Shoo Rayner

*Captain Underpants Series* · *Ricky Ricotta Series*

## Saviour Pirotta
Mythology

Margaret Mayo

Geraldine McCaughrean

*First Greek Myths Series* · *Once Upon a World Series*

## Daniel Postgate
Adventure Family Humour

Mary Hooper

Hilda Offen

*Big Mum Plum!* · *Cosmo and the Pirates* · *Ghost Train*

## Beatrix Potter ○
Animals Family

Nick Butterworth
Joyce Dunbar
Julia Jarman

Arnold Lobel
Jill Tomlinson
Alison Uttley

*The Tale of Benjamin Bunny* · *The Tale of Peter Rabbit*

## Ghillian Potts ○
Magic School

Terence Blacker
Humphrey Carpenter
Maeve Friel
Sam McBratney

Jill Murphy
Wendy Smith
Bob Wilson

*Diary Days* · *A Witch in the Classroom*

## Jillian Powell
Animals Family Humour School

Anne Adeney
Anne Cassidy
John Cunliffe
Penny Dolan
Dave Hanson

Anita Jeram
Karina Law
Nicola Moon
Margaret Nash
Hilary Robinson

*Craig's Crocodile* · *Ellie's Star* · *Izzie's Idea*
*My Nan* · *Ron's Race* · *Tall Tilly*

# Chris Powling

Adventure Family Ghost/supernatural Humour

8-11

Julia Jarman
Margaret Ryan
Dyan Sheldon

Bob Wilson
Philip Wooderson

*A Ghost Behind the Stars* · *Kit's Castle*
*On the Ghost Trail* · *Rover Goes to School*

# Alf Prøysen ⟳

Adventure Fantasy Humour Magic

8-11

Jeff Brown
Megan McDonald

Jeremy Strong

*Mrs Pepperpot Series*

# Shoo Rayner

Adventure Animals Humour

8-11

Jonathan Allen
Harriet Castor
Alan Durant
James Marshall
Dav Pilkey

Alan Rusbridger
Angie Sage
Nick Sharratt
Paul Stewart
Martin Waddell

*Little Horrors Series* · *Millie and Bombassa Series*
*Ricky Rocket Series* · *Scaredy Cats Series*

# Gwyneth Rees ⟳

Magic

8-11

Keith Brumpton
Linda Chapman
Kelly McKain

Daisy Meadows
Hiawyn Oram

*Cosmo and the Magic Sneeze*
*Fairy Dust* · *Mermaid Magic*

# Chris Riddell

Fantasy Humour

Julia Donaldson
Colin McNaughton

Ian Whybrow

*The Emperor of Absurdia*

---

*Go to the back for lists of:*
Authors by Genre · Graphic novels · Prize winners · Exploring further

## Hilary Robinson

Animals Humour

Anne Adeney
Stan and Jan Berenstain
Andy Blackford
Anne Cassidy
Penny Dolan

Dave Hanson
Margaret Nash
Jillian Powell
Nick Sharratt

*Batty Betty's Spells · Croc by the Rock*
*How to Teach a Dragon Manners*
*Pet to School Day · The Royal Jumble Sale*

## Frank Rodgers ⌒

Animals Humour Magic

Scoular Anderson
Marc Brown
Jan Fearnley
Alan Rusbridger

Wendy Smith
Kaye Umansky
Colin West
Jeanne Willis

*Pirate Penguins*
*Little T Series · Mr Croc Series · The Witch's Dog Series*

## Alan Rusbridger ⌒

Animals Humour

Lauren Child
Rose Impey
Julia Jarman
Tony Mitton

Hiawyn Oram
Shoo Rayner
Frank Rodgers

*The Coldest Day at the Zoo*
*The Smelliest Day at the Zoo · The Wildest Day at the Zoo*

## Margaret Ryan ⌒

Adventure Family Humour Magic

8-11

Sally Grindley
Alex Gutteridge
Rose Impey
Ann Jungman
Colin McNaughton

Daisy Meadows
Chris Powling
Dyan Sheldon
Dee Shulman
Karen Wallace

*The Littlest Dragon Gets the Giggles*
*Airy Fairy Series · Fat Alphie and Charlie the Wimp Series*
*Motley's Crew Series*

⌒ Some titles available as **Talking books**

27

5-7

## Louis Sachar    Humour

Jeremy Strong    David Henry Wilson    8-11 12-14
Ian Whybrow

*Marvin Redpost Series*

## Angie Sage    Animals Family Fantasy Humour

Jenny Nimmo    Shoo Rayner    8-11

*Crocodile Canal · The Lonely Puppy · Mouse*

## Dr Seuss ⏳    Humour

Allan Ahlberg    P D Eastman
Stan and Jan Berenstain    Theo Le Sieg
Marc Brown    Colin McNaughton

*The Cat in the Hat · Fox in Socks · Green Eggs and Ham*

## Nick Sharratt    Humour

Giles Andreae    Timothy Knapman
Raymond Briggs    Shoo Rayner
John Grant    Hilary Robinson
Kes Gray    Jeanne Willis

*Caveman Dave · The Green Queen · Monday Run-day*

## Dyan Sheldon ⏳    Adventure Friends Humour School

Jon Blake    Chris Powling    8-11 12-14
Sam McBratney    Margaret Ryan
Marilyn McLaughlin

*Elena the Frog · Leon Loves Bugs*
*Lizzie and Charley Go Away for the Weekend*

## Dee Shulman    Adventure Ghost/supernatural Humour

Scoular Anderson    Margaret Ryan
Julia Jarman    Wendy Smith

*Hetty the Yeti*
*Haunted Mouse Series*

## Francesca Simon 💬

Marc Brown
Ann Cameron
Roald Dahl
Peter Kavanagh
Marilyn McLaughlin

Bel Mooney
Jenny Oldfield
Tony and Jan Payne
Ian Whybrow
David Henry Wilson

*Horrid Henry Series*

## Emily Smith

Ann Cameron
Bob Wilson

Jacqueline Wilson

*Joe vs the Fairies* · *Patrick the Party Hater* · *Robomum*

## Wendy Smith

Scoular Anderson
Terence Blacker
Maeve Friel
Ghillian Potts

Frank Rodgers
Dee Shulman
Kaye Umansky
Jacqueline Wilson

*Mrs Magic Series* · *Space Twins Series*

## Paul Stewart 💬

Scoular Anderson
Damon Burnard
Alan Durant

Shoo Rayner
Jeremy Strong

*Dogbird* · *Dogbird and Other Mixed-up Tales* · *The Were-Pig*
*The Blobheads Series*

## Jeremy Strong 💬

Adrian Boote
Herbie Brennan
Jeff Brown
Keith Brumpton
Roald Dahl

Alf Prøysen
Louis Sachar
Paul Stewart
Jeanne Willis
David Henry Wilson

*Chicken School* · *Dinosaur Pox*
*Giant Jim and the Hurricane* · *My Granny's Great Escape*
*Pirate School Series*

## Jill Tomlinson 💬

Animals  Humour

Phyllis Arkle
Henrietta Branford
Emma Chichester Clark
Peter Clover
Jenny Dale

Pippa Goodhart
Dick King-Smith
Beatrix Potter
Alison Uttley

*The Owl Who Was Afraid of the Dark*
*The Penguin Who Wanted to Find Out*

## Kaye Umansky 💬

Family  Fantasy  Humour  Magic

8-11

Roy Apps
Humphrey Carpenter
Lauren Child
Kes Gray
Tony Mitton

Frank Rodgers
Wendy Smith
Karen Wallace
Jeanne Willis

*The Jealous Giant · Sophie and the Wonderful Picture*
*Buster Gutt Series · Goblinz Series*

## Alison Uttley 💬

Animals

Joyce Dunbar
Beatrix Potter

Jill Tomlinson

*Little Grey Rabbit Series · Sam Pig Series*

## Martin Waddell

Sport

Keith Brumpton
Janet Burchett and Sara Vogler
Rob Childs

Michael Coleman
Shoo Rayner
Bob Wilson

*Cup Final Kid · Cup Run · Going Up · Star Striker Titch*

## Barrie Wade

Fairy/folk  Humour

Anne Adeney
Andy Blackford
Anne Cassidy

Penny Dolan
Dave Hanson
Maggie Moore

*Cinderella · Goldilocks and the Three Bears*
*The Little Mermaid · Rumpelstiltskin · The Three Billy Goats Gruff*

# Karen Wallace 💬     Fairy/folk Family Humour Mythology

8-11 12-14

Scoular Anderson
Roy Apps
Martyn Beardsley
Lisa Bruce
Dennis Hamley

Mary Hooper
Anthony Masters
Margaret Ryan
Kaye Umansky
Philip Wooderson

*Albert's Racoon · Alice Goes to Hollywood · Alice Goes North*
*The Elves and the Shoemaker · The Emperor's New Clothes · Ooh La La Lottie!*
*Sherlock Hound Series · Tales of King Arthur*

# Colin West 💬     Animals Family Humour

Phyllis Arkle
Stan and Jan Berenstain
Andrew Cope
Anita Jeram

Jenny Nimmo
Frank Rodgers
Philip Wooderson

*Big Wig · Moose and Mouse*
*Monty the Dog Series · My Funny Family Series*

# Ian Whybrow 💬     Adventure Animals Humour Letters

8-11

Giles Andreae
Judy Brown
Marc Brown
Damon Burnard
Damian Harvey
Shirley Hughes

Timothy Knapman
Chris Riddell
Louis Sachar
Francesca Simon
David Henry Wilson

*Robin Hood's Best Shot · Tim, Ted and the Pirates · Whizz the Fleabag*
*Books for Boys · Harry Series · Little Wolf Series*

# Jeanne Willis     Animals Death Humour

Scoular Anderson
Damian Harvey
Frank Rodgers

Nick Sharratt
Jeremy Strong
Kaye Umansky

*Mayfly Day*
*Crazy Jobs Series*

# Anna Wilson     Ballet Friends School

8-11

Linda Chapman
Vivian French

Kelly McKain
Daisy Meadows

*Nina Fairy Ballerina*

31

## Bob Wilson
Friends Humour School Sport

Laurence Anholt
Janet Burchett and Sara Vogler
Michael Coleman
Roald Dahl

Ghillian Potts
Chris Powling
Emily Smith
Martin Waddell

*Pump Street Primary Series · Stanley Bagshaw Series*

## David Henry Wilson 💬
Adventure Family Humour

Louis Sachar
Francesca Simon

Jeremy Strong
Ian Whybrow

8-11

*Jeremy James Series*

## Jacqueline Wilson 💬
Adventure Family Fantasy Humour

Malorie Blackman
Anne Fine
Hilary McKay

Bel Mooney
Emily Smith
Wendy Smith

8-11 12-14

*The Monster Storyteller · Monster Eyeballs
My Brother Bernadette · Sleepovers · Werepuppy*

## Philip Wooderson
Adventure Historical Humour

Scoular Anderson
Keith Brumpton
Chris Powling

Karen Wallace
Colin West

*Arf and the Happy Campers GN
Arf and the Tarantula GN · Arf and the Three Dogs GN
The Nile Files Series*

## Chris Wormell
Fairy/folk Fantasy

Laurence Anholt
Julia Donaldson
Emily Gravett

Mini Grey
Oliver Jeffers

*In the Woods · Sea Monster · Two Frogs · The Wild Girl*

## Selina Young
Animals Friends Humour

Tony Bradman
Chris d'Lacey

Vivian French
Arnold Lobel

*Big Dog and Little Dog Go Flying · Big Dog and Little Dog Go Sailing
Big Dog and Little Dog Visit the Moon*

# Authors for Ages 8-11

## Deborah Abela
Adventure  Detective mysteries

Enid Blyton
Carol Hedges
Anthony Masters

Mark McCorkle
Wendelin Van Draanen

*Max Remy: Spyforce Series*

## Richard Adams 💬
Animals  Environment  Fantasy

David Clement-Davies
Colin Dann

Brian Jacques

*Watership Down*

## Allan Ahlberg 💬
Family  Fantasy  Humour

5-7

Giles Andreae
Ian Beck
Simon Mason
Natalie Jane Prior

Alf Prøysen
Shoo Rayner
David Henry Wilson

*The Bear Nobody Wanted*
*The Boy, the Wolf, the Sheep and the Lettuce* · *Woof!*
*The Gaskitts Series*

## Joan Aiken 💬  Adventure  Family  Fantasy  Ghost/supernatural

12-14

Paul Bajoria
Henrietta Branford
Linda Buckley-Archer
Griselda Gifford
Robin Jarvis

Diana Wynne Jones
Garry Kilworth
William Nicholson
Philip Pullman
Celia Rees

*James III Series* · *St Boan Mysteries*

## Louisa May Alcott 💬
Family

Jeanne Birdsall
Frances Hodgson Burnett
Hilary McKay
L M Montgomery

Siobhán Parkinson
Johanna Spyri
Laura Ingalls Wilder

*Good Wives* · *Jo's Boys* · *Little Women*

## David Almond 💬        Family  Fantasy

12-14

Thomas Bloor        Elizabeth Laird
Melvin Burgess       Jan Mark
Berlie Doherty        Andrew Norriss
Sandra Glover        Susan Price
Clive King

*Skellig*

## Rachel Anderson     Family  Illness  Science fiction  War 1939-45

12-14

Julie Bertagna        Michelle Magorian
Sandra Glover        Michael Morpurgo

*Pizza on Saturday* · *Princess Jazz and the Angels*

## Giles Andreae             Humour

5-7

Allan Ahlberg        Shoo Rayner
Martyn Beardsley      Karen Wallace
Natalie Jane Prior

*Luke Lancelot and the Golden Shield*
*Luke Lancelot and the Treasure of the Kings*

## Laurence Anholt 💬         Humour

5-7

Neil Gaiman         Shoo Rayner
Margaret Mahy       Francesca Simon

*Seriously Silly Rhymes Series* · *Seriously Silly Stories Series*

## Roy Apps 💬     Adventure  Fantasy  Historical  Humour

5-7

Morris Gleitzman       Jeremy Strong
Paul Jennings        Alan Temperley

*Anne Frank: the Last Days of Freedom* · *The Time Spinner*
*Stacey Stone Series*

💬 Some titles available as **Talking books**

## Philip Ardagh 💬

Humour

Steve Barlow and Steve Skidmore
Lauren Child
Steve Cole
Morris Gleitzman
Sam Llewellyn

Eric Pringle
Philip Ridley
Lemony Snicket
Cat Weatherill

*The Green Man of Gressingham* BS
*Eddie Dickens Series*
*Unlikely Exploits Series*

## Neil Arksey

Science fiction  Sport

Terence Blacker
Tony Bradman
Rob Childs
Michael Coleman

Chris d'Lacey
Alan Durant
Alan Gibbons

*Brooksie · Fint · MacB · Result · Sudden Death*

## Louise Arnold

Friends  Ghost/supernatural

Bruce Coville
Helen Cresswell
Bridget Crowley
Eva Ibbotson
Tim Kennemore

Penelope Lively
Margaret Mahy
Eric Pringle
Nick Shadow

*The Invisible Friend Series*

## Mary Arrigan 💬   Adventure  Ghost/supernatural  Historical

Alan Garner
Jamila Gavin

Jenny Nimmo
Paul Stewart

*Baldur's Bones · Ghost Bird · Grimstone's Ghost · Lawlor's Revenge*

## Ros Asquith 💬

Friends  Humour

Cathy Cassidy
Yvonne Coppard
Patricia Finney
Mia Ikumi
Karen McCombie

Helena Pielichaty
Gwyneth Rees
Cherry Whytock
Jacqueline Wilson

12-14

*Girl Writer: Castles and Castrophes*
*Fab Four Series · Trixie Tempest, Tweenage Tearaway Series*

8-11

35

8-11

## Steve Augarde
*Fantasy  War*

Holly Black
Malachy Doyle
Sally Gardner
Diana Wynne Jones

Elizabeth Kay
Katherine Langrish
Jenny Nimmo
Terry Pratchett

*Celandine • The Various*

## Paul Bajoria
*Adventure  Historical  Thrillers*

Joan Aiken
Linda Buckley-Archer
Chris Powling

Chris Priestley
Anthony Read
Justin Richards

*The God of Mischief • The Printer's Devil*

## E D Baker
*Magic*

Cressida Cowell
Anna Dale

Jason Hightman
Philip Pullman

*Dragon's Breath • The Frog Princess • Once Upon a Curse*

## Cherith Baldry 💬
*Detective mysteries  Historical: Medieval*

Kevin Crossley-Holland
Caroline Lawrence

Michael Morpurgo
Rosemary Sutcliff

*The Abbey Mysteries Series • Eaglesmount Series*

## Blue Balliett
*Adventure  Detective mysteries  School*

Rick Riordan
Matthew Skelton

Lemony Snicket

*Chasing Vermeer • The Wright 3*

## Lynne Reid Banks 💬
*Family  Fantasy*

Stephen Elboz
Clive King
Penelope Lively

E Nesbit
Mary Norton

12-14

*Harry the Poisonous Centipede*
*Harry the Poisonous Centipede Goes to Sea*
*Harry the Poisonous Centipede's Big Adventure • Tiger, Tiger*
*Indian in the Cupboard Series*

## Antonia Barber 💬

Animals  Ballet  Stage

5-7

Ann Bryant
Adèle Geras

Alexandra Moss
Noel Streatfeild

*The Mousehole Cat*
*Dancing Shoes Series*

## Dominic Barker 💬

Adventure  Detective mysteries
Fantasy  Humour

12-14

Charlie Higson
Anthony Horowitz

Terry Pratchett
Justin Richards

*Blart*

## Steve Barlow and Steve Skidmore 💬

Humour
Mythology

Philip Ardagh
Steve Cole
Roald Dahl
Terry Deary
Andy Griffiths

Mark Haddon
Katherine Langrish
Eric Pringle
John Vornholt

*Mad Myths Series* · *Outernet Series*
*Tales of the Dark Forest Series* · *Vernon Bright Series*

## J M Barrie 💬

Fantasy

Frank L Baum
Lewis Carroll
C S Lewis

Geraldine McCaughrean
P L Travers

*Peter Pan*

## Michelle Bates

Animals

Jenny Dale
Lucy Daniels

Jenny Oldfield

*Sandy Lane Stables Series*

## Frank L Baum 💬

Fantasy

J M Barrie
Lewis Carroll
C S Lewis

Geraldine McCaughrean
P L Travers

*The Wizard of Oz*

## Nina Bawden 💬     Family   War 1939-45

Theresa Breslin
Berlie Doherty
Jackie French
Adèle Geras

Judith Kerr
Michelle Magorian
Linda Newbery

*Carrie's War*

## Martyn Beardsley 💬     Humour

**5-7**

Giles Andreae
Natalie Jane Prior

Shoo Rayner

*Sir Gadabout Series*

## Ian Beck     Fairy/folk   Family

Allan Ahlberg
Heather Dyer

Ted Hughes
Elizabeth Kay

*The Secret History of Tom Trueheart Boy Adventurer*

## David Bedford     Friends   Sport

Bob Cattell

Rob Childs

*The Team Series*

## Julie Bertagna 💬     Animals   Family   Humour   Social issues

**12-14**

Rachel Anderson

Jan Mark

*Dolphin Boy · Ice Cream Machine*
*The Ice Cream Machine Totally Fizzbombed*

## Luc Besson     Fantasy

Holly Black
Herbie Brennan
Eoin Colfer

E Nesbit
Mary Norton
Terry Pratchett

*Arthur and the Forbidden City · Arthur and the Minimoys*

💬 Some titles available as **Talking books**

## Jeanne Birdsall
Family

Louisa May Alcott
Lucy M Boston
Frances Hodgson Burnett

Hilary McKay
L M Montgomery
Siobhán Parkinson

*The Penderwicks*

## Holly Black 〇
Fantasy

12-14

Steve Augarde
Luc Besson
Georgia Byng
Bruce Coville
Malachy Doyle

Sally Gardner
Debi Gliori
Justin Richards
Emily Rodda
Lemony Snicket

*Spiderwick Chronicles*

## Terence Blacker 〇 Adventure Computers Humour Sport

5-7 12-14

Neil Arksey
Malorie Blackman
Tony Bradman

Rob Childs
Michael Coleman
Alan Durant

*The Angel Factory • The Transfer • You Have Ghost Mail*
*Ms Wiz Series*

## Malorie Blackman 〇
Adventure Computers
Detective mysteries Social issues

5-7 12-14

Terence Blacker
Theresa Breslin
Gillian Cross
John Fardell
Alan Gibbons

Sally Grindley
Julia Jarman
Helena Pielichaty
Kate Thompson

*A.N.T.I.D.O.T.E. • Cloud Busting • Dangerous Reality*
*The Deadly Dare Mysteries • Ellie and the Cat • Hostage* BS

## Thomas Bloor
Detective mysteries Family

David Almond
Gillian Cross
Sally Gardner

Lemony Snicket
Robert Swindells

*Beast Beneath the Skin • Blood Willow • Worm in the Blood*

## Judy Blume 💬      Family Humour School

Betsy Byars
Paula Danziger
Anne Fine

Dyan Sheldon
Jacqueline Wilson

*Fudge-a-mania* · *It's Not the End of the World*
*Otherwise Known as Sheila the Great* · *Superfudge*

## Enid Blyton 💬      Adventure Detective mysteries School

Deborah Abela
Elinor M Brent-Dyer
Caroline Lawrence

Anthony Masters
Mary Norton

*Famous Five Series* · *Malory Towers Series* · *Secret Seven Series*

## Michael Bond 💬      Animals Family

Chris d'Lacey
Dick King-Smith

A A Milne

*Olga Da Polga Series* · *Paddington Bear Series*

## Lucy M Boston 💬      Adventure Family Fantasy

Jeanne Birdsall
Frances Hodgson Burnett
Elizabeth Goudge

E Nesbit
Philippa Pearce
P L Travers

*The Children of Green Knowe*
*The Chimneys of Green Knowe* · *The River at Green Knowe*

## Stephen Bowkett      Fantasy

Catherine Fisher
William Nicholson

Philip Reeve

12-14

*Dreamcatcher*
*The Wintering Trilogy*

## Frank Cottrell Boyce 💬 Adventure Crime Family Humour

Morris Gleitzman
Paul Jennings
Andrew Norriss

Philip Ridley
Louis Sachar

12-14

*Framed* · *Millions*

## Tony Bradman
8-11

Adventure Environment Sport
5-7

Neil Arksey
Terence Blacker
Henrietta Branford

Kathryn Cave
Rob Childs
Susan Gates

*Aftershock* · *The Dirty Dozen* BS · *Hurricane* · *The Two Jacks* BS
*Football Fever Series* · *Tales of Terror Series*

## Christiana Brand ⌑

Family Humour

Debi Gliori
Sam Llewellyn

E Nesbit
P L Travers

*Nurse Matilda Series*

## Henrietta Branford ⌑

Adventure Humour
5-7

Joan Aiken
Tony Bradman

Debi Gliori
Jeremy Strong

*Dimanche Diller* · *Dimanche Diller in Danger* · *Dipper's Island*

## Herbie Brennan

Adventure Humour Letters
5-7

Luc Besson
Roald Dahl
Anna Dale
Joseph Delaney
Malachy Doyle

Anthony Horowitz
Daisy Meadows
David Lee Stone
Cat Weatherill

*Faerie Wars* · *The Purple Emperor* · *Ruler of the Realm*

## Elinor M Brent-Dyer ⌑

School

Enid Blyton
Adèle Geras

L M Montgomery

*The Chalet School Series*

## Theresa Breslin ⌑

Fantasy Historical Humour
12-14

Nina Bawden
Malorie Blackman
Berlie Doherty

Caroline Lawrence
J K Rowling
Alan Temperley

*Across the Roman Wall*
*Dream Master Series*

41

## Raymond Briggs 💬
Fantasy  Humour

Neil Gaiman
René Goscinny
Michael Lawrence
Dav Pilkey

5-7

*Fungus the Bogeyman* GN
*Father Christmas* GN · *Jim and the Beanstalk*

## Ann Bryant
Friends  Humour  School

Antonia Barber
Daisy Meadows
Alexandra Moss
Jenny Oldfield
Caroline Plaisted
Noel Streatfeild
Jennie Walters
Holly Webb
Anna Wilson

5-7

*Ballerina Dream Series* · *Make Friends With... Series* · *Step Chain Series*

## Linda Buckley-Archer
Adventure  Historical

Joan Aiken
Paul Bajoria
Helen Cresswell
Chris Priestley
Anthony Read

*Gideon the Cutpurse* · *The Tar Man*

## Melvin Burgess 💬
Fantasy  Ghost/supernatural  Social issues

David Almond
Michael Coleman
Ted Hughes
Jenny Nimmo

12-14

*An Angel for May* · *Copper Treasure* · *The Earth Giant*
*The Ghost Behind the Wall*

## Frances Hodgson Burnett 💬
Family
Historical: Victorian

Louisa May Alcott
Jeanne Birdsall
Lucy M Boston
Elizabeth Goudge
E Nesbit
Gwyneth Rees

*Little Lord Fauntleroy* · *A Little Princess* · *The Secret Garden*

## Betsy Byars 💬
Animals  Family  Humour

Judy Blume
Paula Danziger
Jacqueline Wilson

*The Eighteenth Emergency* · *The Midnight Fox*

## Georgia Byng  Adventure Fantasy Humour Social issues

Holly Black
Lauren Child

Elizabeth Cody Kimmel
Lemony Snicket

*Molly Moon Stops the World* · *Molly Moon's Hypnotic Holiday*
*Molly Moon's Hypnotic Time Travel Adventure*
*Molly Moon's Incredible Book of Hypnotism*

**8-11**

## Lewis Carroll ⌕ Fantasy

J M Barrie
Frank L Baum
C S Lewis

Geraldine McCaughrean
P L Travers

*Alice's Adventures in Wonderland*
*Through the Looking-Glass and What Alice Found There*

## Cathy Cassidy ⌕ Family Social issues Thrillers

Ros Asquith
Hilary McKay

Jacqueline Wilson   12-14

*Driftwood* · *Indigo Blue* · *Scarlett*

## Bob Cattell Other cultures Sport

David Bedford
Rob Childs

Michael Coleman

*Butter-Finger*
*Glory Gardens Series*

## Kathryn Cave Animals Fantasy Humour

Tony Bradman
Steve Cole
Cressida Cowell

Jill Murphy
Eric Pringle

*Henry Hobbs and the Lost Planet* · *Henry Hobbs, Space Voyager*
*Septimus Similon, Practising Wizard*

## Linda Chapman Animals Family Fantasy Magic

Louise Cooper
Annie Dalton
Kathleen Duey

Heather Dyer
Elizabeth Lindsay
Daisy Meadows

5-7

*My Secret Unicorn Series*
*Not Quite a Mermaid Series* · *Stardust Series*

43

## Simon Chapman Adventure

Anthony Horowitz          Robert Westall
Anthony Masters

*Explorers Wanted Series*

## Lauren Child 𝒫 Humour  School

5-7

Philip Ardagh          Jack Gantos
Georgia Byng          Megan McDonald
Yvonne Coppard          Jenny Oldfield

*Clarice Bean Series*

## Rob Childs Sport

5-7

Neil Arksey          Bob Cattell
David Bedford          Michael Coleman
Terence Blacker          Alan Durant
Tony Bradman          Alan Gibbons

*Keeper's Ball · Soccer Shadows · Time and Again*
*Time Ranger Series*

## David Clement-Davies 𝒫 Animals  Fantasy

Richard Adams          Brian Jacques
W J Corbett          Garry Kilworth
Colin Dann          Michelle Paver

*The Alchemists of Barbal · Fire Bringer*
*The Sight · The Telling Pool*

## Steve Cole 𝒫 Humour  Science fiction

Philip Ardagh          Eoin Colfer
Steve Barlow and Steve Skidmore          Sebastian Rook
Kathryn Cave

*Astrosaurs Series · Freakham High Series*

> Go to back for
> lists of:
> Authors by Genre
> Graphic novels
> Prize winners
> Further reading

## Michael Coleman  Adventure Computers Sport

5-7

Neil Arksey
Terence Blacker
Melvin Burgess
Bob Cattell

Rob Childs
Chris d'Lacey
Alan Durant
Alan Gibbons

*Going Straight · Tag · Weirdo's War*
*The Bear Kingdom Trilogy · Internet Detectives Series*

## Eoin Colfer  ⌒  Adventure Detective mysteries Fantasy Humour

12-14

Luc Besson
Steve Cole
Roddy Doyle
Sally Gardner
Debi Gliori

Garry Kilworth
Ian Ogilvy
Terry Pratchett
Philip Ridley
Steve Voake

*Half Moon Investigations · The Legend of Captain Crow's Teeth*
*The Legend of Spud Murphy · The Supernaturalist*
*Artemis Fowl Series*

## Louise Cooper  ⌒  Animals Fantasy Magic

12-14

Linda Chapman
Lucy Daniels

Jenny Oldfield

*Sea Horses · Short and Scary · Short and Spooky*
*Creatures Series*

## Susan Cooper  ⌒  Adventure Fantasy Historical Sea/boats

12-14

Paul Dowswell
Charlie Fletcher
Cornelia Funke
Alan Garner
John Gordon

Geraldine McCaughrean
William Nicholson
Jenny Nimmo
Angie Sage
J R R Tolkien

*The Boggart · Green Boy · Victory*
*The Dark is Rising Series*

## Andrew Cope  Animals Humour

5-7

Joshua Doder
Roddy Doyle

Livi Michael

*Spy Dog · Spy Dog 2*

## Yvonne Coppard
**Family Humour**

Ros Asquith
Lauren Child
Helen Cresswell

Debi Gliori
Meg Harper
Hilary McKay

*Alexandra the Great Series*

## W J Corbett
**Adventure Animals Environment**

David Clement-Davies
Colin Dann
Kenneth Grahame

Brian Jacques
Garry Kilworth

*Last Chance Zoo · Return to the Last Chance Zoo*

## Zizou Corder
**Adventure Animals Fantasy**

Kate di Camillo
Alan Garner
Michael Hoeye

Livi Michael
Daniel Pennac
Alexander McCall Smith

*Lionboy · Lionboy: The Chase · Lionboy: The Truth*

## Bruce Coville
**Fantasy Humour Science fiction**

Louise Arnold
Holly Black
Susan Gates
Simon Goswell

Mark Haddon
Paul Jennings
Michael Lawrence
Justin Richards

*The Magic Shop Series · My Alien Classmate Series*

## Cressida Cowell
**Fantasy Historical Humour Magic**

E D Baker
Kathryn Cave
Chris d'Lacey
Cornelia Funke
Diana Hendry

Jason Hightman
Eva Ibbotson
Jill Murphy
Dugald Steer
Geronimo Stilton

*How to be a Dragon · How to be a Pirate
How to Cheat a Dragon's Curse · How to Speak Dragonese
How to Train Your Dragon*

## Sharon Creech 💬

Diaries Family
Ghost/supernatural Humour

12-14

Kate di Camillo
Berlie Doherty
Sally Grindley

Elmore Leonard
Jan Mark

*The Ghost of Uncle Arvie* · *Love That Dog*
*Granny Torrelli Makes Soup* · *Heartbeat*

## Helen Cresswell 💬

Adventure Family Fantasy Humour

Louise Arnold
Linda Buckley-Archer
Yvonne Coppard
Bridget Crowley
Diana Hendry

Diana Wynne Jones
Penelope Lively
Simon Mason
Philippa Pearce

*Moondial*
*The Bagthorpes Series*

## Richmal Crompton 💬

Family Humour School

René Goscinny
Simon Goswell

Paul Jennings
Francesca Simon

*Just William Series*

## Gillian Cross 💬

Adventure Humour School Thrillers

12-14

Malorie Blackman
Thomas Bloor
Sally Gardner
Anthony Horowitz
Gene Kemp

Jan Mark
Michelle Paver
Bali Rai
Arthur Ransome
Jacqueline Wilson

*The Great Elephant Chase*
*The Monster From the Underground* · *Wolf*
*The Demon Headmaster Series*

## Kevin Crossley-Holland 💬

Adventure Historical: Medieval
Mythology Traditional

12-14

Cherith Baldry
Geraldine McCaughrean
Gerald Morris
William Nicholson
Michelle Paver

Richard Platt
Susan Price
Rick Riordan
Rosemary Sutcliff
T H White

*Arthur Series*

## Bridget Crowley — Ghost/supernatural  Science fiction

Louise Arnold
Helen Cresswell
Penelope Lively
Alexandra Moss

Justin Richards
Nick Shadow
Kate Thompson

*Feast of Fools* · *Harriet's Ghost*

## Chris d'Lacey 💬 — Adventure  Family  Fantasy  Social issues

5-7

Neil Arksey
Michael Bond
Michael Coleman
Cressida Cowell
Alan Durant

Cornelia Funke
Kenneth Grahame
Tim Kennemore
Ian Ogilvy
Steve Voake

*Fire Star* · *The Fire Within* · *Fly Cherokee Fly*
*Horace: a Teddybear Story* · *Icefire* · *Shrinking Ralph Perfect*

## Roald Dahl 💬 — Fantasy  Humour

5-7

Steve Barlow and Steve Skidmore
Herbie Brennan
Eric Pringle

Philip Ridley
Lemony Snicket
Ian Whybrow

*The BFG* · *Charlie and the Chocolate Factory*
*Danny the Champion of the World*
*James and the Giant Peach* · *Matilda*

## Anna Dale 💬 — Adventure  Magic

E D Baker
Herbie Brennan
Joseph Delaney
Maeve Friel
Cornelia Funke

Eva Ibbotson
Jill Marshall
Mark McCorkle
Jill Murphy
Wendelin Van Draanen

*Dawn Undercover* · *Whispering to Witches*

## Jenny Dale 💬 — Animals

5-7

Michelle Bates
Lucy Daniels
Narinder Dhami

Jenny Oldfield
Angie Sage

*Best Friends Series* · *Kitten Tales* · *Puppy Tales*

## Annie Dalton 💬

Family Fantasy

Linda Chapman
Catherine Fisher
Meg Harper
Diana Hendry
Hazel Marshall

Jill Marshall
William Nicholson
Susan Price
Wendelin Van Draanen

*Friday Forever*  BS
*Afterdark Series · Lilac Peabody Series*
*Mel Beeby, Agent Angel Series · Tilly Beaney Series*

## Lucy Daniels 💬

Animals Diaries

5-7

Michelle Bates
Louise Cooper
Jenny Dale
Kathleen Duey

Dick King-Smith
Elizabeth Lindsay
Anna Sewell

*Animal Ark Series*
*Dolphin Diaries Series · Safari Summer Series*

## Colin Dann 💬

Adventure Animals

Richard Adams
David Clement-Davies
W J Corbett
Kenneth Grahame

Brian Jacques
Dick King-Smith
Jenny Oldfield
Dodie Smith

*Animals of Farthing Wood*
*Journey to Freedom · Lion Country*

## Paula Danziger 💬

Family Humour

Judy Blume
Betsy Byars
Mary Hooper
Megan McDonald

Helena Pielichaty
Dyan Sheldon
Francesca Simon

*The Cat Ate My Gymsuit*
*A is for Amber Series*

BS = Published by Barrington Stoke
specialists in resources for dyslexic and struggling readers

## Terry Deary 💬 Historical Humour Mythology War 1939-45

Steve Barlow and Steve Skidmore
René Goscinny
Caroline Lawrence
Gerald Morris

Richard Platt
Rick Riordan
Dugald Steer

*The Fire Thief* · *Flight of the Fire Thief* · *Ghost for Sale* BS
*The Hat Trick* BS · *Pitt Street Pirates* BS · *War Games* BS
*Horrible Histories Series* · *The Tudor Chronicles*

## Joseph Delaney 💬 Ghost/supernatural Magic

12-14

Herbie Brennan
Anna Dale
Jeanne DuPrau
Diana Wynne Jones

Sebastian Rook
Angie Sage
J R R Tolkien

*The Spook's Apprentice*
*The Spook's Curse* · *The Spook's Secret*

## Narinder Dhami 💬 Animals School Sport

12-14

Jenny Dale
Rose Impey

Hilary McKay
Jacqueline Wilson

*Changing Places* · *Grow Up Dad!* BS · *Sunita's Secret*

## Kate di Camillo Animals Family Other lands

Zizou Corder
Sharon Creech

Michael Hoeye

*Because of Winn-Dixie* · *The Miraculous Journey of Edward Tulane*
*The Tale of Despereaux* · *The Tiger Rising*

## Joshua Doder Animals Humour

Andrew Cope
Roddy Doyle

Livi Michael
Kaye Umansky

*A Dog Called Grk*
*Grk and the Hot Dog Trail* · *Grk and the Pelotti Gang*

*Go to back for lists of:*
Authors by Genre · Graphic novels · Prize winners · Exploring further

## Berlie Doherty 🗩 Adventure Family Fantasy Historical

David Almond
Nina Bawden
Theresa Breslin
Sharon Creech
Anne Fine

Sandra Glover
Penelope Lively
Geraldine McCaughrean
Linda Newbery
Philippa Pearce

12-14

*Granny Was a Buffer Girl*
*The Sailing Ship Tree* · *The Starbuster*

## Paul Dowswell Historical: Victorian Sea/boats War

Susan Cooper
Elizabeth Laird

Michael Molloy

12-14

*The Adventures of Sam Witchall*

## Malachy Doyle 🗩 Fantasy

Steve Augarde
Holly Black

Herbie Brennan

5-7

*Amadans* · *Amadans Alert*

## Roddy Doyle 🗩 Animals Humour

Eoin Colfer
Andrew Cope

Joshua Doder
Jeremy Strong

*The Giggler Treatment*
*The Meanwhile Adventures* · *Rover Saves Christmas*

## Kathleen Duey Animals Fantasy

Linda Chapman
Lucy Daniels

Elizabeth Lindsay

*The Unicorn's Secret Series*

## Fiona Dunbar Family Magic

Anne Fine
Rose Impey
Karen McCombie

Gwyneth Rees
Margaret Ryan
Jacqueline Wilson

*Chocolate Wishes* · *Cupid Cakes* · *The Truth Cookie*

## Helen Dunmore ✎
Adventure Family Friends School

Anne Fine
Lesley Howarth

Siobhán Parkinson

5-7

*Ingo* · *The Lilac Tree*
*Seal Cove* · *The Silver Bead* · *The Tide Knot*

## Jeanne DuPrau
Fantasy Science fiction

Joseph Delaney
Cornelia Funke

Livi Michael
Angie Sage

*The City of Ember*
*The People of Sparks* · *The Prophet of Yonwood*

## Alan Durant ✎
Adventure Humour Sport

Neil Arksey
Terence Blacker
Rob Childs

Michael Coleman
Chris d'Lacey

5-7

*Game Boy* BS · *Game Boy Reloaded* BS · *Stat Man* BS
*Bad Boyz Series* · *Creepe Hall Series* · *Leggs United Series*

## Heather Dyer ✎
Humour Magic

Ian Beck
Linda Chapman

Eva Ibbotson
Gwyneth Rees

*The Fish in Room 11* · *The Girl With the Broken Wing*

## Stephen Elboz
Fantasy Magic

Lynne Reid Banks
Cornelia Funke
Diana Hendry

Diana Wynne Jones
J K Rowling
Steve Voake

12-14

*A Wild Kind of Magic*
*A Store of Secrets* [originally published as *The Byzantium Bazaar*]
*Ghostlands* · *The Prisoner's Apprentice* · *The Tower at Moonville*

## John Fardell
Adventure

Malorie Blackman

Julia Jarman

*The Flight of the Silver Turtle*
*The Seven Professors of the Far North*

## Anne Fine 💬

Diaries  Family  Humour  School

5-7 12-14

Judy Blume
Berlie Doherty
Fiona Dunbar
Helen Dunmore
Pippa Goodhart

Lesley Howarth
Gene Kemp
Karen McCombie
Helena Pielichaty
Jacqueline Wilson

8-11

*Charm School* · *Frozen Billy* · *Goggle Eyes*
*How to Write Really Badly* · *Jennifer's Diary* · *The More the Merrier*

## Patricia Finney

Diaries  Historical: Tudor

Ros Asquith
Julia Golding
Mary Hooper

Richard Platt
Karen Wallace

*Lady Grace Mysteries*

## Catherine Fisher 💬

Fantasy  Thrillers

12-14

Stephen Bowkett
Annie Dalton
Alan Garner
Robin Jarvis
Diana Wynne Jones

Garry Kilworth
William Nicholson
Michelle Paver
Katherine Roberts
Val Tyler

*The Archon* · *The Oracle* · *The Scarab*
*Book of the Crow Series* · *The Snow Walker Series*

## Charlie Fletcher 💬

Fantasy  Friends

12-14

Susan Cooper
Alan Garner
C S Lewis

E Nesbit
Robert Westall

*Stone Heart*

## Jackie French

School  War 1939-45

Nina Bawden
Anne Holm
Judith Kerr

Ian Serraillier
Robert Westall

*Dark Wind Blowing* · *Hitler's Daughter*

## Maeve Friel 💬     Magic

**5-7**

Anna Dale
Eva Ibbotson
Daisy Meadows

Jill Murphy
Gwyneth Rees

*Witch in Training Series*

## Cornelia Funke 💬     Adventure Fantasy

Susan Cooper
Cressida Cowell
Chris d'Lacey
Anna Dale
Jeanne DuPrau

Stephen Elboz
Jason Hightman
Eva Ibbotson
J K Rowling

*Dragon Rider · Inkheart · Inkspell · The Thief Lord*

## Neil Gaiman     Fantasy Humour

**5-7**

Laurence Anholt

Raymond Briggs

*The Day I Swapped My Dad for Two Goldfish*
*Wolves in the Walls*

## Jack Gantos     Family School Social issues

Lauren Child
Morris Gleitzman
Gene Kemp

Andrew Norriss
Louis Sachar

*Joey Pigza Loses Control*
*Joey Pigza Swallowed the Key · What Would Joey Do?*

## Sally Gardner 💬     Historical Magic

**5-7 12-14**

Steve Augarde
Holly Black
Thomas Bloor
Eoin Colfer

Gillian Cross
Mary Hooper
Theresa Tomlinson

*I, Coriander*

Go to back for lists of:
Authors by Genre · Graphic novels · Prize winners · Exploring further

## Alan Garner 💬         Adventure  Fantasy

Mary Arrigan
Susan Cooper
Zizou Corder
Catherine Fisher
Charlie Fletcher

John Gordon
Diana Wynne Jones
Philip Pullman
J R R Tolkien
T H White

*A Bag of Moonshine* · *Elidor*
*The Moon of Gomrath* · *The Weirdstone of Brisingamen*
*The Stone Book Quartet*

## Susan Gates 💬      Adventure  Family  Fantasy  Humour

12-14

Tony Bradman
Bruce Coville
Andy Griffiths

Mark Haddon
Michael Lawrence
Dav Pilkey

*A Brief History of Slime* · *Firebird* · *The Ice Thief*
*Return of the Mad Mangler* · *The Spud from Outer Space*

## Jamila Gavin         Family  Fantasy  Other lands

5-7 12-14

Mary Arrigan
Adèle Geras

Julia Jarman

*Danger By Moonlight* · *Deadly Friend* · *From Out of the Shadows*
*Grandpa Chatterji* · *Grandpa Chatterji's Indian Summer*
*Grandpa Chatterji's Third Eye*

## Adèle Geras              Ballet  Family

5-7 12-14

Antonia Barber
Nina Bawden
Elinor M Brent-Dyer

Jamila Gavin
Alexandra Moss
Noel Streatfeild

*Apricots at Midnight* · *The Gingerbread House* BS
*Lizzie's Wish* · *Louisa the Ballerina*

## Alan Gibbons       Fantasy  Social issues  Sport

12-14

Neil Arksey
Malorie Blackman
Rob Childs

Michael Coleman
Diana Hendry
Paul Shipton

*Ganging Up*
*The Legendeer Trilogy* · *Total Football Series*

## Griselda Gifford

Ghost/supernatural
Social issues  War 1939-45

Joan Aiken
Penelope Lively
Margaret Mahy

Jenny Nimmo
Robert Swindells

*House of Spies · Second Sight · The Silent Pool*

## Morris Gleitzman 💬  Animals  Family  Humour  War 1939-45

12-14

Roy Apps
Philip Ardagh
Frank Cottrell Boyce
Jack Gantos
Mark Haddon

Harry Horse
Paul Jennings
Michael Lawrence
Sam Llewellyn

*Aristotle's Nostril · Boy Overboard · Girl Underground
Once · Teacher's Pet · Worm Story*

## Debi Gliori 💬

Family  Fantasy  Humour  Magic

Holly Black
Christiana Brand
Henrietta Branford
Eoin Colfer
Yvonne Coppard

Kes Gray
Nigel Hinton
Sam Llewellyn
Terry Pratchett
Margaret Ryan

*Deep Fear · Deep Trouble · Deep Water
Pure Dead Brilliant · Pure Dead Gorgeous*

## Sandra Glover

Friends  Thrillers

David Almond
Rachel Anderson

Berlie Doherty

12-14

*Deadline · Demon's Rock · My Spooky Sister*

## Julia Golding

Fantasy  Stage

Patricia Finney
John Gordon
Matthew Skelton

Noel Streatfeild
Karen Wallace

*Cat Among the Pigeons · The Den of Thieves
The Diamond of Drury Lane
The Gorgon's Gaze · Secret of the Sirens*

## Pippa Goodhart

Animals  Ghost/supernatural

Anne Fine                    Michael Morpurgo

*Connor's Eco Den*  BS  ·  *The House With No Name*  BS
*Ratboy*  BS  ·  *Slow Magic*

## John Gordon

Fantasy  Ghost/supernatural

Susan Cooper                 Julia Golding
Alan Garner

*The Giant Under the Snow*

## René Goscinny 💬

Historical: Roman  Humour

Raymond Briggs               Andrew Norriss
Richmal Crompton             Dav Pilkey
Terry Deary                  Jeremy Strong
Hergé                        Willy Vandersteen

*Asterix Series*  GN

## Simon Goswell

Fantasy

Bruce Coville                Paul Jennings
Richmal Crompton

*Theo Slugg in Dead Trouble*  ·  *Theo Slugg in Low Spirits*

## Elizabeth Goudge 💬

Fantasy

Lucy M Boston                E Nesbit
Frances Hodgson Burnett

*The Little White Horse*

## Kenneth Grahame 💬

Animals  Fantasy

W J Corbett                  Brian Jacques
Chris d'Lacey                Dick King-Smith
Colin Dann                   A A Milne

*The Reluctant Dragon*  ·  *The Wind in the Willows*

GN = Graphic Novel

## Kes Gray 💬
Fantasy  Humour

5-7

Debi Gliori
Eva Ibbotson

Paul Shipton
Kaye Umansky

*Nelly the Monster Sitter Series*

## Andy Griffiths
Humour

Steve Barlow and Steve Skidmore
Susan Gates
Michael Lawrence

Dav Pilkey
Jamie Rix

*Bum Series* • *Just Series*

## Sally Grindley 💬  Family  Letters  Other cultures  War 1939-45

5-7

Malorie Blackman
Sharon Creech
Julia Jarman
Elizabeth Laird

Helena Pielichaty
Jean Ure
Ian Whybrow

*Bravo Max* • *Dear Max* • *Feather Wars* • *Spilled Water*

## Mark Haddon 💬
Humour  Space

12-14

Steve Barlow and Steve Skidmore
Bruce Coville
Susan Gates
Morris Gleitzman

Sam Llewellyn
Philip Ridley
Louis Sachar

*Agent Z Series*

## Dennis Hamley
War 1939-45

5-7

Jan Mark
Linda Newbery

Ian Serraillier
Robert Westall

*The Diary of a World War II Pilot* • *The War and Freddy*

## Meg Harper 💬
Friends  Humour

Yvonne Coppard
Annie Dalton

Diana Hendry
Karen McCombie

*My Mum is... Series* • *Saint Jenni Series*

💬 Some titles available as Talking books

## Carol Hedges Adventure

Deborah Abela
Charlie Higson

Jill Marshall
Mark McCorkle

*Spy Girl Series*

## Diana Hendry 🗩 Family Fantasy Social issues

Cressida Cowell
Helen Cresswell
Annie Dalton
Stephen Elboz

Alan Gibbons
Meg Harper
Jill Murphy
J K Rowling

*Catch A Gran* BS · *The Crazy Collector*
*Harvey Angell and the Ghost Child*
*Swan Boy* · *You Can't Kiss it Better*

## Hergé 🗩 Adventure Historical

René Goscinny
Charlie Higson
Gerald Morris

Joshua Mowll
Willy Vandersteen

*Tintin* GN

## Jason Hightman 🗩 Adventure Fantasy

E D Baker
Cressida Cowell

Cornelia Funke
William Nicholson

*The Saint of Dragons* · *Samurai*

## Charlie Higson 🗩 Adventure

Dominic Barker
Carol Hedges
Hergé

Anthony Horowitz
Mark McCorkle
Joshua Mowll

12-14

*Young Bond Series*

## Nigel Hinton 🗩 Adventure Fantasy

Debi Gliori
Mary Norton

Robert C O'Brien

12-14

*Time Bomb*
*Beaver Towers Series*

## Michael Hoeye

Zizou Corder
Kate di Camillo
Brian Jacques
Robin Jarvis
Garry Kilworth

Dick King-Smith
Ian Ogilvy
S F Said
E B White

*No Time Like Show Time*
*The Sands of Time* · *Time Stops for No Mouse*

## Anne Holm ⌒
War 1939-45

Jackie French
Judith Kerr
Ian Serraillier

Sandi Toksvig
Robert Westall

*I Am David*

## Mary Hooper ⌒
Animals  Ghost/supernatural
Historical  Humour
5-7 12-14

Paula Danziger
Patricia Finney
Sally Gardner

Margaret Mahy
Dyan Sheldon
Jean Ure

*The Genie* BS · *Haunted House* · *Horror House*
*Neighbourhood Witch* · *Plague House* · *Witch House*
*Lucy's Farm Series*

## Anthony Horowitz ⌒
Adventure  Humour
12-14

Dominic Barker
Herbie Brennan
Simon Chapman
Gillian Cross
Charlie Higson

Harry Horse
Joshua Mowll
Philip Ridley
Nick Shadow
Ian Whybrow

*Granny* · *Groosham Grange* · *Return to Groosham Grange*
*The Switch* · *The Unholy Grail: a Tale of Groosham Grange*
*The Diamond Brothers Series*

## Harry Horse ⌒
Letters

Morris Gleitzman

Anthony Horowitz

*The Last Castaways* · *The Last Cowboys*
*The Last Gold Diggers* · *The Last Polar Bears*

8-11

## Lesley Howarth 💬

Fantasy   Science fiction   Social issues

12-14

Helen Dunmore
Anne Fine
Andrew Norriss

Siobhán Parkinson
Celia Rees

*Calling the Shots · I Managed a Monster · Mister Spaceman*

## Ted Hughes 💬

Environment   Fantasy   Mythology

Ian Beck
Melvin Burgess
Clive King

Geraldine McCaughrean
Robert C O'Brien

*The Dreamfighter and Other Creation Tales*
*How the Whale Became and Other Stories*
*The Iron Man · The Iron Woman*

## Eva Ibbotson 💬

Adventure   Fantasy
Ghost/supernatural   Humour

12-14

Louise Arnold
Cressida Cowell
Anna Dale
Heather Dyer
Maeve Friel

Cornelia Funke
Kes Gray
Tim Kennemore
Emily Rodda
Kate Saunders

*The Beasts of Clawstone Castle · The Great Ghost Rescue*
*Journey to the River Sea · The Secret of Platform 13*
*The Star of Kazan · Which Witch*

## Mia Ikumi

Environment   Fantasy   Friends

Ros Asquith
Jill Marshall

Jacqueline Wilson

*Tokyo Mew Mew* GN

## Rose Impey 💬

Family   Humour

5-7

Narinder Dhami
Fiona Dunbar
Karen McCombie
Barbara Mitchelhill

Gwyneth Rees
Margaret Ryan
Jean Ure

*Hot House Flower*
*My Scary Fairy Godmother · The Shooting Star*

## Steve Jackson and Ian Livingstone

Katherine Roberts

Emily Rodda

*Fighting Fantasy Series*

## Brian Jacques 💬

Adventure  Animals  Fantasy

12-14

Richard Adams
David Clement-Davies
W J Corbett
Colin Dann
Kenneth Grahame

Michael Hoeye
Robin Jarvis
Garry Kilworth
Robert C O'Brien
S F Said

*Redwall Series*

## Julia Jarman 💬

Family  Ghost/supernatural  Historical

5-7

Malorie Blackman
John Fardell
Jamila Gavin

Sally Grindley
Caroline Lawrence
Paul Shipton

*Ghost Writer* · *The Jessame Stories*
*The Time-travelling Cat Series*

## Robin Jarvis 💬

Fantasy

12-14

Joan Aiken
Catherine Fisher
Michael Hoeye
Brian Jacques

Livi Michael
Robert C O'Brien
S F Said

*The Deptford Histories Series* · *The Mouselets of Deptford Series*
*Tales from the Wyrd Museum Series* · *The Whitby Witches Series*

## Cindy Jefferies

School

Kelly McKain
Alexandra Moss

Helena Pielichaty
Caroline Plaisted

*Fame School Series*

GN = Graphic Novel

## Paul Jennings 💬

**Fantasy   Humour**

8-11

Roy Apps
Frank Cottrell Boyce
Bruce Coville
Richmal Crompton
Morris Gleitzman

Simon Goswell
Dav Pilkey
Philip Ridley
Jeremy Strong
Ceri Worman

12-14

*Come Back Gizmo · Sink the Gizmo*

## Pete Johnson 💬

**Ghost/supernatural   Humour   Thrillers**

Allan Frewin Jones
Anthony Masters

R L Stine
Robert Swindells

12-14

*Avenger · Help I'm a Classroom Gambler · Hero Game*
*How to Train Your Parents · Trust Me I'm a Troublemaker*

## Allan Frewin Jones 💬

**Adventure   Detective mysteries**

Pete Johnson
Anthony Masters

Robert Swindells

*Talisman Series*

## Diana Wynne Jones 💬

**Fantasy   Ghost/supernatural   Magic**

Joan Aiken
Steve Augarde
Helen Cresswell
Joseph Delaney
Stephen Elboz

Catherine Fisher
Alan Garner
Elizabeth Kay
J K Rowling

12-14

*The Chrestomanci Series*

## Elizabeth Kay

**Fantasy   Magic**

Steve Augarde
Ian Beck

Diana Wynne Jones
Jenny Nimmo

*Back to the Divide · The Divide · Jinx on the Divide*

💬 Some titles available as **Talking books**

63

## Gene Kemp

Humour  School

Gillian Cross
Anne Fine
Jack Gantos

Hilary McKay
Catherine MacPhail

*Nothing Scares Me*
*Seriously Weird* · *The Turbulent Term of Tyke Tyler*

## Tim Kennemore

Family  Magic

Louise Arnold
Chris d'Lacey

Eva Ibbotson

*Alice's Birthday Pig* · *Alice's Shooting Star*
*Alice's World Record* · *Circle of Doom* · *Sabine*

## Deborah Kent

Animals  Historical

Elizabeth Lindsay
Jenny Oldfield

Anna Sewell

*Saddle the Wind Series*

## Judith Kerr

War 1939-45

Nina Bawden
Jackie French
Anne Holm
Michelle Magorian

Linda Newbery
Ian Serraillier
Sandi Toksvig
Robert Westall

*Bombs on Aunt Dainty* · *A Small Person Far Away*
*When Hitler Stole Pink Rabbit*

## P B Kerr

Adventure  Fantasy

Hazel Marshall
Kenneth Oppel

Cat Weatherill

*Children of the Lamp Series*

## Garry Kilworth

Adventure  Animals
Detective mysteries  Fantasy

Joan Aiken
David Clement-Davies
Eoin Colfer
W J Corbett

Catherine Fisher
Michael Hoeye
Brian Jacques
Michelle Paver

*The Gargoyle* · *Night Dancer* · *Silver Claw*
*The Welkin Weasels Series*

## Elizabeth Cody Kimmel

Georgia Byng                    Helena Pielichaty
Siobhán Parkinson

*Lily B on the Brink of Cool*
*Lily B on the Brink of Love* · *Lily B on the Brink of Paris*

## Clive King 💬

Adventure Environment

David Almond                    Andrew Norriss
Lynne Reid Banks               Robert C O'Brien
Ted Hughes                      Arthur Ransome

*Stig of the Dump*

## Dick King-Smith 💬

Animals Family Humour

Michael Bond          Livi Michael          5-7
Lucy Daniels          Jenny Oldfield
Colin Dann            Dodie Smith
Kenneth Grahame       Geronimo Stilton
Michael Hoeye         E B White

*Billy the Bird* · *The Crowstarver*
*Harry's Mad* · *Just Binnie*

## Elizabeth Laird 💬

Adventure Family
Other cultures Social issues

David Almond          Michael Molloy        12-14
Paul Dowswell         Michael Morpurgo
Sally Grindley        Alexander McCall Smith

*The Garbage King* · *Paradise End*
*Red Sky in the Morning*
*Secret Friends* · *Secrets of the Fearless*

## Katherine Langrish 💬

Fairy/folk Fantasy
Historical: Vikings

Steve Augarde                   Paul Stewart
Steve Barlow and Steve Skidmore  John Vornholt
Ian Ogilvy

*Troll Blood* · *Troll Fell* · *Troll Mill*

## Caroline Lawrence  💬 Detective mysteries  Historical: Roman

Cherith Baldry
Enid Blyton
Theresa Breslin
Terry Deary
Julia Jarman

Joshua Mowll
Katherine Roberts
Paul Shipton
Rosemary Sutcliff

*The Roman Mysteries Series*

## Michael Lawrence  Fantasy  Humour

Raymond Briggs
Bruce Coville
Susan Gates
Morris Gleitzman

Andy Griffiths
Dav Pilkey
Jamie Rix

12-14

*The Griffin and Oliver Pie*
*Young Dracula* BS · *Young Monsters* BS
*Jiggy McCue Series*

## Elmore Leonard 💬  Animals  Fantasy

Sharon Creech

Daniel Pennac

*A Coyote's in the House*

## C S Lewis 💬  Fantasy

J M Barrie
Frank L Baum
Lewis Carroll
Charlie Fletcher

E Nesbit
Philip Pullman
J R R Tolkien
T H White

*Chronicles of Narnia*

## Elizabeth Lindsay  Animals  Magic

Linda Chapman
Lucy Daniels
Kathleen Duey

Deborah Kent
Jenny Oldfield
Anna Sewell

5-7

*Magic Pony Series*

BS = Published by Barrington Stoke
specialists in resources for dyslexic and struggling readers

66

## Penelope Lively 💬     Adventure   Fantasy   Ghost/supernatural

8-11

Louise Arnold
Lynne Reid Banks
Helen Cresswell
Bridget Crowley

Berlie Doherty
Griselda Gifford
Philippa Pearce

*The Ghost of Thomas Kempe*

## Sam Llewellyn 💬     Adventure   Horror   Humour

Philip Ardagh
Christiana Brand
Morris Gleitzman
Debi Gliori

Mark Haddon
Joshua Mowll
Lemony Snicket

*Bad Bad Darlings* · *Desperado Darlings* · *Little Darlings*
*The Haunting of Death Eric* · *The Return of Death Eric*

## Geraldine McCaughrean 💬     Fairy/folk   Fantasy   Historical   Other lands

5-7 12-14

J M Barrie
Frank L Baum
Lewis Carroll
Susan Cooper
Kevin Crossley-Holland

Berlie Doherty
Ted Hughes
Michael Morpurgo
Theresa Tomlinson

*Mo* · *Not the End of the World* · *Peter Pan in Scarlet*
*The Questing Knights of the Faerie Queen* · *Smile*

## Karen McCombie 💬     Family   Friends   Humour

12-14

Ros Asquith
Fiona Dunbar
Anne Fine
Meg Harper
Rose Impey

Hilary McKay
Gwyneth Rees
Margaret Ryan
Cherry Whytock

*Ally's World Series* · *Indie Kidd Series* · *Stella etc Series*

## Mark McCorkle     Adventure

Deborah Abela
Anna Dale
Carol Hedges

Charlie Higson
Jill Marshall

*Kim Possible Series* GN

## Megan McDonald 💬      Family Humour

5-7

Lauren Child      Gwyneth Rees
Paula Danziger      Francesca Simon
Shoo Rayner

*Judy Moody Series · Stink Series*

## Kelly McKain      Diaries Friends Humour School

5-7

Cindy Jefferies      Bali Rai
Hilary McKay      Margaret Ryan
Alexandra Moss

*Pony Camp Diaries · Totally Lucy Series*

## Hilary McKay 💬      Family Humour Social issues

5-7 12-14

Louisa May Alcott      Gene Kemp
Jeanne Birdsall      Karen McCombie
Cathy Cassidy      Kelly McKain
Yvonne Coppard      Simon Mason
Narinder Dhami      Barbara Mitchelhill

*Caddy Ever After · The Exiles*
*Indigo's Star · Permanent Rose · Saffy's Angel*

## Catherine MacPhail      Family Humour Social issues

12-14

Gene Kemp      Jan Mark

*Catch us if you Can · Get That Ghost to Go!* BS
*Picking on Percy* BS *· Traitor's Gate* BS
*Granny Nothing Series*

## Michelle Magorian 💬      Family War 1939-45

12-14

Rachel Anderson      Philippa Pearce
Nina Bawden      Ian Serraillier
Judith Kerr      Sandi Toksvig
Linda Newbery      Robert Westall

*Back Home · Goodnight Mister Tom*

---

GN = Graphic Novel
BS = Published by Barrington Stoke
specialists in resources for dyslexic and struggling readers

---

## Margaret Mahy 💬

Adventure Family
Ghost/supernatural Humour
12-14

Laurence Anholt
Louise Arnold
Griselda Gifford
Mary Hooper

Philip Ridley
Ursula Moray Williams
David Henry Wilson

*The Haunting · The Gargling Gorilla and other Stories
The Riddle of the Frozen Phantom*

## Jan Mark 💬

Family Humour Social issues
12-14

David Almond
Julie Bertagna
Sharon Creech
Gillian Cross

Dennis Hamley
Catherine MacPhail
Andrew Norriss

*Eyes Wide Open · King John and the Abbott
Lady Long-legs · Robin Hood all at Sea* BS

## Hazel Marshall 💬

Fantasy Historical

Annie Dalton
P B Kerr

Paul Stewart

*Troublesome Angels Series*

## Jill Marshall 💬

Adventure

Anna Dale
Annie Dalton
Carol Hedges
Charlie Higson

Mia Ikumi
Mark McCorkle
Wendelin Van Draanen

*Jane Blonde Series*

## Simon Mason 💬

Family Humour

Allan Ahlberg
Helen Cresswell

Hilary McKay
Louis Sachar

*The Quigleys Series*

Go to back for lists of:
Authors by Genre · Graphic novels · Prize winners · Exploring further

8-11

## Anthony Masters 💬 Adventure Animals Ghost/supernatural

5-7 12-14

Deborah Abela
Enid Blyton
Simon Chapman
Pete Johnson
Allan Frewin Jones

Nick Shadow
R L Stine
Robert Swindells
Robert Westall

*Beware the Wicked Web*
*Freddy's Fox* GN · *Tod and the Sand Pirates* BS
*Predator Series*

## Daisy Meadows 💬 Friends Magic

5-7

Herbie Brennan
Ann Bryant
Linda Chapman
Maeve Friel

Gwyneth Rees
Margaret Ryan
Anna Wilson

*The Jewel Fairies* · *The Party Fairies*
*The Pet Keeper Fairies* · *The Weather Fairies*

## Livi Michael 💬 Animals Fantasy Humour

Andrew Cope
Zizou Corder
Joshua Doder
Jeanne DuPrau
Robin Jarvis

Dick King-Smith
Michael Molloy
Cat Weatherill
Ian Whybrow

*43, Bin Street*
*Seventeen Times as High as the Moon* · *The Whispering Road*
*Frank and the .... Series*

## A A Milne 💬 Animals

Michael Bond

Kenneth Grahame

*The House at Pooh Corner* · *Winnie the Pooh*

## Barbara Mitchelhill Detective mysteries Family Humour

5-7

Rose Impey
Hilary McKay

Philip Ridley

*How to be a Detective* · *Kids on the Run* · *Spycatcher*
*Eric Series*

## Michael Molloy  Adventure Fantasy Historical: Victorian Sea/boats

12-14

Paul Dowswell
Elizabeth Laird

Livi Michael
Justin Somper

*House on Falling Star Hill · Peter Raven Under Fire*
*Witch Trade Trilogy*

## L M Montgomery 💬  Family

Louisa May Alcott
Jeanne Birdsall
Elinor M Brent-Dyer

Johanna Spyri
Laura Ingalls Wilder

*Anne of Avonlea · Anne of Green Gables · Anne of the Island*

## Michael Morpurgo 💬  Adventure Historical
Social issues War 1939-45

5-7 12-14

Rachel Anderson
Cherith Baldry
Pippa Goodhart
Elizabeth Laird
Geraldine McCaughrean

Gerald Morris
Jenny Nimmo
Philippa Pearce
Sandi Toksvig
T H White

*Alone on a Wide Wide Sea · The Amazing Story of Adolphus Tips*
*The Best Christmas Present in the World · Fox Friend* BS
*I Believe In Unicorns · Sir Gawain & the Green Knight*

## Gerald Morris  Fairy/folk Historical: Medieval

Kevin Crossley-Holland
Terry Deary

Hergé
Michael Morpurgo

*The Squire's Tales Series*

## Alexandra Moss  Ballet Diaries School

Antonia Barber
Ann Bryant
Bridget Crowley
Adèle Geras

Cindy Jefferies
Kelly McKain
Noel Streatfeild
Anna Wilson

*The Royal Ballet School Diaries*

💬 Some titles available as **Talking books**

71

## Joshua Mowll — Adventure  Family  Fantasy  Other cultures

Hergé
Charlie Higson
Anthony Horowitz
Caroline Lawrence

Sam Llewellyn
Chris Priestley
Robert Swindells

12-14

*Operation Red Jericho • Operation Typhoon Shore*

## Jill Murphy 💬 — Fantasy  Humour  Magic  School

Kathryn Cave
Cressida Cowell
Anna Dale
Maeve Friel
Diana Hendry

Natalie Jane Prior
J K Rowling
Louis Sachar
Kate Saunders
Kaye Umansky

5-7

*The Worst Witch Series*

## E Nesbit 💬 — Family  Fantasy

Lynne Reid Banks
Luc Besson
Lucy M Boston
Christiana Brand

Frances Hodgson Burnett
Charlie Fletcher
Elizabeth Goudge
C S Lewis

*Five Children and It
The Phoenix and the Carpet • The Railway Children*

## Linda Newbery — Animals  Family  Social issues  War 1939-45

Nina Bawden
Berlie Doherty
Dennis Hamley

Judith Kerr
Michelle Magorian
Ian Serraillier

12-14

*At the Firefly Gate • Blitz Boys
Catcall • Lost Boy • Polly's March*

## William Nicholson 💬 — Adventure  Fantasy

Joan Aiken
Stephen Bowkett
Susan Cooper
Kevin Crossley-Holland
Annie Dalton

Catherine Fisher
Jason Hightman
Kenneth Oppel
Philip Reeve

12-14

*Wind on Fire Trilogy*

## Jenny Nimmo 💬

Family Fantasy
Ghost/supernatural Science fiction
5-7

| | |
|---|---|
| Mary Arrigan | Elizabeth Kay |
| Steve Augarde | Michael Morpurgo |
| Melvin Burgess | Stephen Potts |
| Susan Cooper | J K Rowling |
| Griselda Gifford | Val Tyler |

*The Night of the Unicorn · The Witch's Tears*
*Children of the Red King Series · The Snow Spider Trilogy*

**8-11**

## Andrew Norriss 💬 Family Fantasy Humour Science fiction

| | |
|---|---|
| David Almond | Lesley Howarth |
| Frank Cottrell Boyce | Clive King |
| Jack Gantos | Jan Mark |
| René Goscinny | |

*Aquila · Matt's Million*
*The Touchstone · The Unluckiest Boy in the World*

## Mary Norton 💬 Adventure Family Fantasy

| | |
|---|---|
| Lynne Reid Banks | Alf Prøysen |
| Luc Besson | P L Travers |
| Enid Blyton | Cat Weatherill |
| Nigel Hinton | |

*Bedknob and Broomstick · The Borrowers*
*The Borrowers Afield · The Borrowers Afloat · The Borrowers Aloft*

## Robert C O'Brien 💬 Environment Fantasy

| | |
|---|---|
| Nigel Hinton | Robin Jarvis |
| Ted Hughes | Clive King |
| Brian Jacques | |

*Mrs Frisby and the Rats of Nimh*

## Ian Ogilvy Fantasy Humour

| | |
|---|---|
| Eoin Colfer | Rick Riordan |
| Chris d'Lacey | Paul Stewart |
| Michael Hoeye | David Lee Stone |
| Katherine Langrish | E B White |

*Measle and the Dragodon · Measle and the Mallockee*
*Measle and the Slithergoul · Measle and the Wrathmonk*

# Jenny Oldfield 💬    Animals Family Humour Pony/horse

5-7

Michelle Bates
Ann Bryant
Lauren Child
Louise Cooper
Jenny Dale

Colin Dann
Deborah Kent
Dick King-Smith
Elizabeth Lindsay
Angie Sage

*Harmony Harris Cuts Loose*
*Definitely Daisy Series · Dreamseeker Trilogy*
*Home Farm Twins Series*
*Horses of Half Moon Ranch Series · My Magical Pony Series*

# Kenneth Oppel 💬 Adventure Animals Fantasy Social issues

P B Kerr
William Nicholson

Philip Reeve
Justin Somper

*Airborn · Firewing · Skybreaker*

# Siobhán Parkinson    Family Friends Humour

Louisa May Alcott
Jeanne Birdsall
Helen Dunmore

Lesley Howarth
Elizabeth Cody Kimmel
Helena Pielichaty

*Four Kids, Three Cats, Two Cows, One Witch (maybe)*
*Second Fiddle · Something Invisible*

# Michelle Paver 💬    Animals Fantasy

12-14

David Almond
David Clement-Davies
Gillian Cross
Kevin Crossley-Holland
Catherine Fisher

Garry Kilworth
Daniel Pennac
J K Rowling
Paul Stewart
J R R Tolkien

*Wolf Brother · Soul Eater · Spirit Walker*

# Philippa Pearce 💬    Adventure Animals Family Fantasy

Lucy M Boston
Helen Cresswell
Berlie Doherty
Penelope Lively

Michelle Magorian
Michael Morpurgo
Arthur Ransome
Sandi Toksvig

*The Battle of Bubble and Squeak · A Dog So Small*
*The Little Gentleman · Minnow on the Say*
*Tom's Midnight Garden · The Way to Sattin Shore*

## Daniel Pennac Animals

Zizou Corder
Elmore Leonard

Michelle Paver
S F Said

*Dog · Eye of the Wolf · Kamo's Escape*

## Helena Pielichaty

Diaries Friends Letters School

8-11

12-14

Ros Asquith
Malorie Blackman
Paula Danziger
Anne Fine
Sally Grindley

Cindy Jefferies
Elizabeth Cody Kimmel
Siobhán Parkinson
Bali Rai
Cherry Whytock

*There's Only One Danny Ogle*
*After School Club Series · Simone Series*

## Dav Pilkey

Humour

5-7

Raymond Briggs
Susan Gates
René Goscinny
Andy Griffiths
Paul Jennings

Michael Lawrence
Jamie Rix
David Roberts
Francesca Simon

*Captain Underpants Series · Ricky Ricotta Series*

## Caroline Plaisted

Friends

12-14

Ann Bryant
Cindy Jefferies
Jean Ure

Jennie Walters
Holly Webb

*Do I Look Like I Care?*
*Glitter Girls Series*

## Richard Platt

Diaries Historical

Kevin Crossley-Holland
Terry Deary
Patricia Finney

Dugald Steer
Karen Wallace

*Castle Diary · Egyptian Diary · Pirate Diary*

## Stephen Potts
Adventure Fantasy Sea/boats Social issues

David Almond

Jenny Nimmo

*Abigail's Gift · Compass Murphy*
*Hunting Gumnor · The Ship Thief*

8-11

## Chris Powling
Adventure

Paul Bajoria
Chris Priestley
Alexander McCall Smith

Jeremy Strong
Karen Wallace

5-7

*Best in the World* BS

## Terry Pratchett ⬭
Fantasy Humour

Steve Augarde
Dominic Barker
Luc Besson
Eoin Colfer

Debi Gliori
Philip Ridley
Paul Stewart
David Lee Stone

12-14

*The Amazing Maurice and His Educated Rodents*
*The Carpet People · A Hat Full of Sky*
*The Bromiliad Trilogy · Johnny Maxwell Stories*

## Susan Price
Fantasy Ghost/supernatural

David Almond
Kevin Crossley-Holland

Annie Dalton
Celia Rees

12-14

*Foiling the Dragon · The Ghost Drum · Ghost Song*
*Hairy Bill · Telling Tales · The Wolf's Footprint*
*Olly Spellmaker Series*

## Chris Priestley
Adventure Detective mysteries
Historical Thrillers

Paul Bajoria
Linda Buckley-Archer
Joshua Mowll

Chris Powling
Philip Pullman
Anthony Read

*Tom Marlowe Series*

Go to back for lists of:
Authors by Genre · Graphic novels · Prize winners · Exploring further

## Eric Pringle 💬

Fairy/folk  Humour

Philip Ardagh
Louise Arnold
Steve Barlow and Steve Skidmore

*Big George*
*Big George and the Seventh Knight*
*Big George and the Winter King*

Kathryn Cave
Roald Dahl

## Natalie Jane Prior 💬

Adventure  Humour

Allan Ahlberg
Giles Andreae

Martyn Beardsley
Jill Murphy

*Lily Quench Series*

## Alf Prøysen 💬

Magic

5-7

Allan Ahlberg
Mary Norton

Ursula Moray Williams

*Mrs Pepperpot Stories*

## Philip Pullman 💬

Adventure  Fairy/folk  Fantasy

12-14

Joan Aiken
E D Baker
Alan Garner
C S Lewis
Chris Priestley

Anthony Read
Philip Reeve
Justin Richards
J R R Tolkien

*Aladdin and the Enchanted Lamp*
*Count Karlstein, or the Ride of the Demon Huntsman*
*The Firework-maker's Daughter*
*I Was a Rat! ...or The Scarlet Slippers*
*The Scarecrow and His Servant*
*His Dark Materials Trilogy*

## Bali Rai 💬

Friends  Other cultures  School

12-14

Gillian Cross
Kelly McKain

Helena Pielichaty
Jacqueline Wilson

*Tales From Devana High Series*

💬 Some titles available as **Talking books**

77

**8-11**

## Arthur Ransome                        Adventure  Family

Gillian Cross                    Philippa Pearce
Clive King

*Swallows and Amazons Series*

## Shoo Rayner                                    Humour

Allan Ahlberg            Martyn Beardsley          5-7
Giles Andreae           Megan McDonald
Laurence Anholt         Louis Sachar

*Ricky Rocket Series · Scaredy Cats Series*

## Anthony Read          Detective mysteries  Historical: Victorian

Paul Bajoria                 Philip Pullman
Linda Buckley-Archer         Justin Richards
Chris Priestley              Bowering Sivers

*The Baker Street Boys Series*

## Celia Rees          Fantasy  Ghost/supernatural  Social issues

Joan Aiken                   Susan Price              12-14
Lesley Howarth

*The Bailey Game · The Cunning Man*

## Gwyneth Rees                          Fairy/folk  Magic

Ros Asquith                  Rose Impey               5-7
Frances Hodgson Burnett      Karen McCombie
Fiona Dunbar                 Megan McDonald
Heather Dyer                 Daisy Meadows
Maeve Friel                  Jean Ure

*Cosmo and the Great Witch Escape · Fairy Gold*
*Fairy Treasure · The Making of May*
*The Mum Detective · My Mum's From Planet Pluto*

Go to back for
lists of:
Authors by Genre
Graphic novels
Prize winners
Further reading

# Philip Reeve 💬

Adventure  Humour

Stephen Bowkett
William Nicholson
Kenneth Oppel

Philip Pullman
Paul Stewart

12-14

*Larklight*
*Buster Bayliss Series*

# Justin Richards 💬

Adventure  Detective mysteries
Historical  Science fiction

Paul Bajoria
Dominic Barker
Holly Black
Bruce Coville
Bridget Crowley

Philip Pullman
Anthony Read
Bowering Sivers
Karen Wallace

*Dr Who* · *The Invisible Detective Series*

# Philip Ridley 💬

Family  Fantasy  Humour

Philip Ardagh
Frank Cottrell Boyce
Eoin Colfer
Roald Dahl
Mark Haddon

Anthony Horowitz
Paul Jennings
Margaret Mahy
Barbara Mitchelhill
Terry Pratchett

*Kasper in the Glitter* · *Krindle Krax* · *Mighty Fizz Chilla*
*Vinegar Street* · *Zinder Zunder* · *Zip's Apollo*

# Rick Riordan

Adventure  Humour  Mythology

Blue Balliett
Kevin Crossley-Holland
Terry Deary

Ian Ogilvy
Katherine Roberts
Paul Shipton

*Percy Jackson and the Lightning Thief*
*Percy Jackson and the Sea of Monsters*

# Jamie Rix 💬

Diaries  Humour

Andy Griffiths
Michael Lawrence

Dav Pilkey
Jeremy Strong

*The War Diaries of Alistair Fury*

# David Roberts

Dav Pilkey

Louis Sachar

Francesca Simon

*Dirty Bertie Series*

# Katherine Roberts
Adventure  Fantasy  Mythology

Catherine Fisher

Steve Jackson and
  Ian Livingstone

Caroline Lawrence

Rick Riordan

Emily Rodda

Paul Shipton

Dugald Steer

J R R Tolkien

12-14

*The Echorium Sequence*
*The Seven Fabulous Wonders Series*

# Emily Rodda
Adventure  Detective mysteries  Fantasy

Holly Black

Eva Ibbotson

Steve Jackson and
  Ian Livingstone

Katherine Roberts

*Deltora Quest Series*

# Sebastian Rook
Adventure  Horror  Thrillers

Steve Cole

Joseph Delaney

Justin Somper

*Vampire Plagues Series*

# J K Rowling ⌒
Fantasy  Magic  School

Theresa Breslin

Stephen Elboz

Cornelia Funke

Diana Hendry

Diana Wynne Jones

Jill Murphy

Jenny Nimmo

Michelle Paver

Kaye Umansky

12-14

*Harry Potter Series*

⌒ Some titles available as **Talking books**

## Margaret Ryan 💬

Family Humour

5-7

Fiona Dunbar
Debi Gliori
Rose Impey
Karen McCombie

Kelly McKain
Daisy Meadows
Kate Saunders
Jean Ure

*Operation Wedding* · *Wild Kat McCrumble*
*Airy Fairy Series*

## Louis Sachar 💬

Humour School Social issues

5-7 12-14

Frank Cottrell Boyce
Jack Gantos
Mark Haddon
Simon Mason

Jill Murphy
Shoo Rayner
David Roberts
Francesca Simon

*Holes* · *Small Steps*
*Marvin Redpost Series* · *Wayside School Series*

## Angie Sage

Animals Magic

5-7

Richard Adams
Susan Cooper
Jenny Dale
Joseph Delaney

Jeanne DuPrau
Jenny Oldfield
Lemony Snicket

*Flyte* · *Magyk*
*Araminta Spook Series*

## S F Said

Animals Science fiction

Michael Hoeye
Brian Jacques

Robin Jarvis
Daniel Pennac

*The Outlaw Varjak Paw* · *Varjak Paw*

## Kate Saunders

Fantasy

Eva Ibbotson
Jill Murphy

Margaret Ryan

*Cat and the Stinkwater War* · *The Little Secret*
*The Belfry Witches Series*

Go to back for lists of:
Authors by Genre · Graphic novels · Prize winners · Exploring further

## Ian Serraillier 💬      War 1939-45

Jackie French      Michelle Magorian
Dennis Hamley      Linda Newbery
Anne Holm      Robert Westall
Judith Kerr

*The Silver Sword*

## Anna Sewell 💬      Animals  Pony/horse

Lucy Daniels      Elizabeth Lindsay
Deborah Kent

*Black Beauty*

## Nick Shadow      Horror

12-14

Louise Arnold      Anthony Horowitz
Bridget Crowley      Anthony Masters

*Midnight Library Series*

## Dyan Sheldon 💬      Adventure  Humour

5-7 12-14

Judy Blume      Mary Hooper
Paula Danziger

*Lizzie and Charlie Go Away for the Weekend*
*Undercover Angel Strikes Again • What Mona Wants, Mona Gets*

## Paul Shipton 💬      Historical  Humour  Mythology

Alan Gibbons      Caroline Lawrence
Kes Gray      Rick Riordan
Julia Jarman      Katherine Roberts

*The Pig Scrolls • The Pig That Saved the World*
*Bug Muldoon Series*

## Francesca Simon 💬      Family  Humour

5-7

Laurence Anholt      David Roberts
Richmal Crompton      Louis Sachar
Paula Danziger      Jean Ure
Megan McDonald      David Henry Wilson
Dav Pilkey

*The Horrid Henry Series*

## Bowering Sivers Adventure  Historical: Victorian

Anthony Read                    Lemony Snicket
Justin Richards

*Jammy Dodgers Get Filthy Rich*
*Jammy Dodgers Go Underground* · *Jammy Dodgers On The Run*

## Matthew Skelton Fantasy

Blue Balliett                    Julia Golding

*Endymion Spring*

## Alexander McCall Smith Animals  Detective mysteries<br>Humour  Other cultures

Zizou Corder                    Chris Powling
Elizabeth Laird                 Karen Wallace

*The BubbleGum Tree* · *The Doughnut Ring*
*The Popcorn Pirates* · *The Spaghetti Tangle*
*Akimbo Series* · *Harriet Bean Series*

## Dodie Smith 🗨 Adventure  Animals

Colin Dann                      E B White
Dick King-Smith

*One Hundred and One Dalmatians* · *The Starlight Barking*

## Lemony Snicket 🗨 Fantasy  Humour

Philip Ardagh                   Roald Dahl
Blue Balliett                   Sam Llewellyn
Holly Black                     Angie Sage
Thomas Bloor                    Bowering Sivers
Georgia Byng                    R L Stine

*A Series of Unfortunate Events*

## Justin Somper Fantasy  Horror

Michael Molloy                  Sebastian Rook
Kenneth Oppel                   R L Stine
Philip Reeve

*Vampirates Series*

# Johanna Spyri 💬 Family

Louisa May Alcott          Laura Ingalls Wilder
L M Montgomery

*Heidi*

8-11

# Dugald Steer Historical  Magic

12-14
Cressida Cowell            Richard Platt
Terry Deary                Katherine Roberts

*Dragonology · Piratology · Wizardology*

# Paul Stewart 💬 Animals  Fantasy

5-7
Mary Arrigan               Terry Pratchett
Katherine Langrish         Philip Reeve
Hazel Marshall             David Lee Stone
Ian Ogilvy                 Val Tyler
Michelle Paver             Steve Voake

*The Edge Chronicles Series*
*Far Flung Adventures Series · Free Lance Series*

# Geronimo Stilton Animals  Humour

Cressida Cowell            Ian Whybrow
Dick King-Smith

*Geronimo Stilton Series*

# R L Stine Horror

12-14
Pete Johnson               Lemony Snicket
Anthony Masters            Justin Somper

*Goosebumps Series*

# David Lee Stone 💬 Fantasy

12-14
Herbie Brennan             Terry Pratchett
Ian Ogilvy                 Paul Stewart

*The Illmoor Chronicles*

💬 Some titles available as **Talking books**

# Noel Streatfeild $\wp$

Ballet  Family  Stage

Antonia Barber
Ann Bryant
Adèle Geras

Julia Golding
Alexandra Moss

*Ballet Shoes · Ballet Shoes for Anna*

# Jeremy Strong $\wp$

Family  Humour

5-7 12-14

Roy Apps
Henrietta Branford
Roddy Doyle
René Goscinny
Paul Jennings

Chris Powling
Jamie Rix
Ian Whybrow
David Henry Wilson
Ceri Worman

*The Beak Speaks · Chicken School · Let's Do the Pharoah*
*My Brother's Famous Bottom Gets Pinched*
*Return of the Hundred-mile-an-hour Dog*
*Wanted! The Hundred-mile-an-hour Dog*

# Rosemary Sutcliff

Historical: Medieval, Roman
Mythology

Cherith Baldry
Kevin Crossley-Holland
Caroline Lawrence

Theresa Tomlinson
T H White

*Beowulf: Dragonslayer*
*Black Ships Before Troy · The High Deeds of Finn MacCool*
*The Eagle of the Ninth Sequence · The King Arthur Trilogy*

# Robert Swindells $\wp$

Adventure  Ghost/supernatural
Science fiction  War 1939-45

12-14

Thomas Bloor
Griselda Gifford
Pete Johnson
Allan Frewin Jones
Anthony Masters

Joshua Mowll
Alan Temperley
Kate Thompson
Robert Westall

*Blitzed · Jacqueline Hyde · Room 13*
*The Thousand Eyes of Night · Timesnatch*

# Alan Temperley $\wp$

Adventure  Fantasy  Horror  Magic

Roy Apps
Theresa Breslin

Robert Swindells

*Harry and the Treasure of Eddie Carver*
*The Magician of Samarkand · Rag Boy*

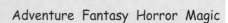

## Kate Thompson 💬 Fantasy Ghost/supernatural

Malorie Blackman    Robert Swindells    12-14
Bridget Crowley

*The Missing Link Trilogy* · *The Switchers Trilogy*

## Sandi Toksvig Other cultures War 1939-45

Anne Holm    Michael Morpurgo
Judith Kerr    Philippa Pearce
Michelle Magorian

*Hitler's Canary* · *Super-saver-mouse to the Rescue*

## J R R Tolkien 💬 Adventure Fantasy

Susan Cooper    Michelle Paver    12-14
Joseph Delaney    Philip Pullman
Alan Garner    Katherine Roberts
C S Lewis

*The Hobbit* GN · *The Lord of the Rings*

## Theresa Tomlinson Family Fantasy Historical Social issues

Sally Gardner    Rosemary Sutcliff    12-14
Geraldine McCaughrean

*Against the Tide* · *Dancing Through the Shadows*
*Scavenger Boy* · *The Voyage of the Silver Bream*

## P L Travers 💬 Family Fantasy Humour Magic

J M Barrie    Christiana Brand
Frank L Baum    Lewis Carroll
Jeanne Birdsall    Mary Norton
Lucy M Boston

*Mary Poppins Series*

## Val Tyler Fantasy

Catherine Fisher    Paul Stewart
Jenny Nimmo

*Time Wreccas* · *The Time Apprentice*

## Kaye Umansky 💬
Humour  Magic

5-7

Joshua Doder
Kes Gray
Jill Murphy

J K Rowling
Jean Ure
David Henry Wilson

*Meet the Weirds* BS · *Mick McMenace, Ghost Detective*
*The Silver Spoon of Solomon Snow*
*Solomon Snow and the Stolen Jewel* · *Wilma's Wicked Spell*
*Goblinz Series* · *Pongwiffy Series*

8-11

## Jean Ure 💬
Diaries  Ghost/supernatural  Letters  School

12-14

Sally Grindley
Mary Hooper
Rose Impey
Caroline Plaisted
Gwyneth Rees

Margaret Ryan
Francesca Simon
Kaye Umansky
Jacqueline Wilson

*Boys Beware* · *Is Anybody There?* · *Over the Moon*
*Secret Life of Sally Tomato* · *Secret Meeting* · *Sugar and Spice*
*Girlfriends Series* · *Sandy Simmons Series*

## Wendelin Van Draanen
Detective mysteries  Humour

Deborah Abela
Anna Dale

Annie Dalton
Jill Marshall

*Sammy Keyes Series*

## Willy Vandersteen
Adventure

René Goscinny

Hergé

*The Greatest Adventures of Spike and Suzy* GN

## Steve Voake
Fantasy

Eoin Colfer
Chris d'Lacey

Stephen Elboz
Paul Stewart

*Daisy Dawson*
*Dreamwalker's Child* · *Web of Fire*

> GN = Graphic Novel
> BS = Published by Barrington Stoke
> specialists in resources for dyslexic and struggling readers

## John Vornholt
Fantasy

Steve Barlow and Steve Skidmore    Katherine Langrish

*The Troll King Trilogy*

## Karen Wallace
Adventure  Historical

5-7 12-14

Giles Andreae              Chris Powling
Patricia Finney           Justin Richards
Julia Golding             Alexander McCall Smith
Richard Platt

*Crunchbone Castle Chronicles · Lady Violet Winters Case Book*

## Jennie Walters
Friends

12-14

Ann Bryant              Holly Webb
Caroline Plaisted

*Party Girls Series*

## Cat Weatherill
Adventure  Fantasy  Magic

Philip Ardagh           Livi Michael
Herbie Brennan       Mary Norton
P B Kerr

*Barkbelly · Snowbone*

## Holly Webb
Friends

Ann Bryant              Jennie Walters
Caroline Plaisted

*Triplets Series*

## Robert Westall 💬
Adventure  Ghost/supernatural
War 1939-45

12-14

Simon Chapman       Judith Kerr
Charlie Fletcher      Michelle Magorian
Jackie French         Anthony Masters
Dennis Hamley       Ian Serraillier
Anne Holm            Robert Swindells

*Blitz · The Creature in the Dark*
*The Machine Gunners · Stormsearch · A Time of Fire*

## E B White 💬

Michael Hoeye
Dick King-Smith
Ian Ogilvy

Dodie Smith
Ursula Moray Williams

*Charlotte's Web* · *Stuart Little*

**8-11**

## T H White

Fantasy Mythology

Kevin Crossley-Holland
Alan Garner
C S Lewis

Michael Morpurgo
Rosemary Sutcliff

*The Sword in the Stone*

## Ian Whybrow 💬

Diaries Humour Letters

Roald Dahl
Sally Grindley
Anthony Horowitz

Livi Michael
Geronimo Stilton
Jeremy Strong

5-7

*Muckabout School* · *The Unvisibles*
*Little Wolf Series*

## Cherry Whytock

Friends

Ros Asquith
Karen McCombie

Helena Pielichaty

*Cherry Faberoony Fizzy Pink* · *Fizzy Pink*
*Angel Series*

## Laura Ingalls Wilder 💬

Family Other lands

Louisa May Alcott
Susan M Coolidge

L M Montgomery
Johanna Spyri

*The Little House in the Big Woods*
*The Little House on the Prairie* · *On the Banks of Plum Creek*

## Ursula Moray Williams 💬  Adventure Animals Fantasy

Margaret Mahy
Alf Prøysen

E B White

*Adventures of the Little Wooden Horse*
*Gobbolino: the Witch's Cat*

## Anna Wilson
Ballet  Friends  School

5-7

Ann Bryant
Daisy Meadows

Alexandra Moss

*Nina Fairy Ballerina Series*

## David Henry Wilson ⌐
Humour

5-7

Allan Ahlberg
Margaret Mahy
Francesca Simon

Jeremy Strong
Kaye Umansky

*Jeremy James Series*

## Jacqueline Wilson ⌐
Family  Humour  Social issues

5-7 12-14

Ros Asquith
Judy Blume
Betsy Byars
Cathy Cassidy
Gillian Cross
Narinder Dhami

Fiona Dunbar
Anne Fine
Mia Ikumi
Bali Rai
Jean Ure

*Best Friends · Candy Floss · Clean Break*
*Diamond Girls · Midnight · Starring Tracy Beaker*

## Ceri Worman ⌐
Humour

Paul Jennings

Jeremy Strong

*The Secret Life of Jamie B*

⌐ Some titles available as **Talking books**

*Go to back for*
*lists of:*
Authors by Genre
Graphic novels
Prize winners
Further reading

# Authors for Ages 12-14

## Joan Aiken 💬
**Adventure Fantasy Ghost/supernatural Historical**

8-11

Louise Cooper          Robin Jarvis
Ann Halam              Ben Jeapes
Frances Hardinge       Diana Wynne Jones

*The Witch of Clatteringshaws*
*The Wolves of Willoughby Chase Series · James III Series*

2-14

## Lloyd Alexander
**Fantasy**

N M Browne            Garth Nix
Alison Croggon        Jonathan Stroud

*The Chronicles of Prydain Series*

## Alison Allen-Gray
**Family Mystery Science fiction**

David Belbin          James Patterson
Terence Blacker       Marc Sumerak
Patrick Cave          Scott Westerfeld
Alan Gibbons          Tim Wynne-Jones

*Unique*

## David Almond 💬
**Family Fantasy Ghost/supernatural Social issues**

8-11

Tim Bowler            Susan Price
Cathy Cassidy         Louis Sachar
Sandra Glover         Marcus Sedgwick
Sonya Hartnett        John Singleton
Nicola Morgan         Robert Swindells

*Clay · The Fire-Eaters · Skellig*

## Rachel Anderson
**Family Illness Social issues War**

8-11

Theresa Breslin       Michelle Magorian
Sandra Glover         Michael Morpurgo
Ann Halam             Linda Newbery
Frances Mary Hendry   Alison Prince

*Joe's Story* BS *· The Rattletrap Trip*
*Red Moon · This Strange New Life · Warlands*
*Moving Times Trilogy*

## Bernard Ashley
**Family  Social issues  Thrillers  War**

Veronica Bennett
Anne Cassidy
Berlie Doherty

Catherine MacPhail
Jan Mark
Matt Whyman

*Down to the Wire* · *Playing Against the Odds* BS
*Smokescreen* · *Ten Days to Zero* · *Torrent* BS

12-14

## Sherry Ashworth
**Friends  Social issues  Thrillers**

Kevin Brooks
Alan Gibbons
Philip Gross

Sue Mayfield
Rosie Rushton

*Disconnected* · *Paralysed* · *Something Wicked*

## Ros Asquith
**Family  Humour  Romance  School**

8-11

Meg Cabot
Cathy Cassidy
Josephine Feeney
Kathryn Lamb
Sue Limb

Karen McCombie
Caroline Plaisted
Chloë Rayban
Louise Rennison
Jean Ure

*Love, Fifteen*
*The Teenage Worrier Guides Series*

## Lynne Reid Banks  ⬭  Other cultures  Other lands  Social issues

8-11

Sharon Creech
Elizabeth Laird
Joan Lingard

Beverley Naidoo
Suzanne Fisher Staples
Tim Wynne-Jones

*The Dungeon* · *Stealing Stacey* · *Tiger, Tiger*

## Dominic Barker  ⬭  Detective mysteries  Fantasy  Humour

8-11

David Belbin

Charlie Higson

*Blart*
*Mickey Sharp Series*

## Raffaella Barker  ⬭  Family  Friends  School

Anne Cassidy
Susan Juby
Hope Larson

Chloë Rayban
Catherine Robinson
Jacqueline Wilson

*Phosphorescence*

# Joan Bauer
**Family Friends Social issues**

Tim Bowler
Joan O'Neill

Catherine Robinson
Meg Rosoff

*Hope Was Here · Rules of the Road*

# David Belbin
**Adventure Social issues Thrillers**

Alison Allen-Gray
Dominic Barker
Malorie Blackman
Melvin Burgess
Charlie Higson

Anthony Horowitz
Sam Hutton
Penny Kendal
Nicola Morgan
M E Rabb

*Coma* BS · *Festival* · *Nicked* BS
*The Beat Series*

# Veronica Bennett
**Family Romance School Social issues**

Bernard Ashley
Malorie Blackman
Anne Fine
Nigel Hinton

Pete Johnson
Brian Keaney
Karen Wallace

*Angelmonster · The Boy-free Zone · Cassandra's Sister · Fish Feet*

# Julie Bertagna
**Environment Fantasy Social issues**

8-11

Terence Blacker
Melvin Burgess
Patrick Cave
Anne Fine
Adèle Geras

Julia Green
Lesley Howarth
Catherine MacPhail
Celia Rees

*Bungee Hero* BS · *Exodus*
*The Opposite of Chocolate · Soundtrack · Zenith*

# Holly Black
**Fantasy**

8-11

Trudi Canavan
Stephen Cole
Alison Croggon

Marianne Curley
Sally Gardner
Tamora Pierce

*Tithe · Valiant*

BS = Published by Barrington Stoke
specialists in resources for dyslexic and struggling readers

## Terence Blacker 🗩 Computers  Science fiction  Social issues

Alison Allen-Gray
Julie Bertagna

Malorie Blackman    5-7 8-11
Pete Johnson

*The Angel Factory* · *Boy 2 Girl* · *Parent Swap*

## Malorie Blackman 🗩 Computers  Family  Social issues  Thrillers

David Belbin
Veronica Bennett
Terence Blacker
Anne Cassidy
Helena Pielichaty

Chloë Rayban    5-7 8-11
Celia Rees
Nicky Singer
Mildred D Taylor
Kate Thompson

*Dead Gorgeous*
*Noughts and Crosses Trilogy*

**12–14**

## Martin Booth 🗩
Adventure  Historical  Thrillers
War 1939-45

Michael Cronin
Michael Morpurgo
Linda Newbery

James Riordan
Robert Swindells
Robert Westall

*Coyote Moon* · *Dr Illuminatus* · *Midnight Saboteur* · *Soul Stealer*

## Stephen Bowkett
Fantasy

William Nicholson

Philip Reeve    8-11

*Dreamcatcher*
*The Wintering Trilogy*

## Tim Bowler
Family  Social issues

David Almond
Joan Bauer
Kevin Brooks
Gillian Cross
Catherine Forde

Sonya Hartnett
Brian Keaney
Graham Marks
Valerie Mendes
Tom Pow

*Apocalypse* · *Blood on Snow* · *Frozen Fire*
*Starseeker* · *Storm Catchers* · *Walking With the Dead*

> 🗩 Some titles available as Talking books

## Frank Cottrell Boyce 💭 Detective mysteries  Family  Humour

8-11

Anne Cassidy
Gennifer Choldenko
Anne Fine

Mark Haddon
Eva Ibbotson
Paul Jennings

*Framed · Millions*

## John Boyne 💭 Death  Social issues  War 1939-45

Michael Cronin
Morris Gleitzman
Michael Morpurgo

Jerry Spinelli
Suzanne Fisher Staples
Markus Zusak

*The Boy in the Striped Pyjamas*

## Ann Brashares Friends

Meg Cabot
Cathy Hopkins
Karen McCombie

Joan O'Neill
Catherine Robinson

*Girls in Pants · The Second Summer of the Sisterhood*
*Sisterhood of the Travelling Pants*

## Theresa Breslin Family  Fantasy  Social issues  War 1914-18

8-11

Rachel Anderson
Sharon Creech
Michael Cronin
Berlie Doherty
Adèle Geras

Joan Lingard
Michelle Magorian
Joan O'Neill
Meg Rosoff

*Divided City · The Medici Seal · Mutant* BS
*Prisoner in Alcatraz* BS *· Remembrance · Saskia's Journey*

## Kevin Brooks Family  Mystery  Social issues

Sherry Ashworth
Tim Bowler
Melvin Burgess
Catherine Forde
Alan Gibbons

Keith Gray
Sonya Hartnett
Anthony McGowan
Nicky Singer
Matt Whyman

*Bloodline* BS *· I See You, Baby*
*Kissing the Rain* BS *· Martyn Pig · The Road of the Dead*

12-14

## N M Browne
Fantasy  Historical: Roman  Mythology

Lloyd Alexander
Alison Croggon
Kevin Crossley-Holland

Marianne Curley
Catherine Fisher
Katherine Roberts

*Basilisk* · *Hunted* · *The Story of Stone*
*Warriors of Alavna* · *Warriors of Camlann*

## Melvin Burgess ⌐
Family  Mythology  Science fiction
Social issues
8-11

David Belbin
Julie Bertagna
Kevin Brooks
Anne Cassidy
Susan Gates

Keith Gray
Lian Hearn
S E Hinton
Penny Kendal

*Billy Elliot* · *Bloodsong* · *Bloodtide*

**12-14**

## A J Butcher
Adventure  Thrillers

Charlie Higson
Anthony Horowitz
Sam Hutton
Andy McNab and Robert Rigby

Robert Muchamore
M E Rabb
Malcolm Rose
Chris Ryan

*Spy High Series*

## Meg Cabot ⌐
Detective mysteries  Diaries  Friends  Humour

Ros Asquith
Ann Brashares
Kate Cann
Cathy Hopkins

Kathryn Lamb
Andrew Matthews
M E Rabb
Louise Rennison

*All American Girl* · *All American Girl: Ready or Not*
*Avalon High* · *Nicola and the Viscount* · *Teen Idol*
*Mediator Series* · *Missing Series* · *Princess Diaries Series*

## Trudi Canavan ⌐
Fantasy  Magic

Holly Black
Alison Croggon
Marianne Curley
Garth Nix

Christopher Paolini
Tamora Pierce
Katherine Roberts
G P Taylor

*The Black Magician Trilogy*

## Kate Cann 💬      Family  Friends  Social issues

Meg Cabot      Cathy Hopkins
Mary Hooper      Karen McCombie

*Crow Girl* BS · *Fiesta* · *Leaving Poppy* · *Text Game* BS

## Anne Cassidy 💬    Detective mysteries  Social issues  Thrillers

5-7

Bernard Ashley      Catherine Forde
Raffaella Barker      Mark Haddon
Malorie Blackman      Meg Rosoff
Frank Cottrell Boyce      Robert Swindells
Melvin Burgess      Lee Weatherly

*Blood Money* BS · *Looking for JJ*
*Love Letters* · *Missing Judy* · *Tough Love* · *Witness* BS

## Cathy Cassidy 💬      Family  Social issues  Thrillers

8-11

David Almond      Hilary McKay
Ros Asquith      Rosie Rushton
Kathryn Lamb      Jean Ure
Sue Limb      Jacqueline Wilson

*Dizzy* · *Driftwood* · *Indigo Blue*

## Patrick Cave 💬      Social issues  Thrillers

Alison Allen-Gray      Philip Gross
Julie Bertagna      Malcolm Rose
Gillian Cross

*Blown Away* · *Last Chance* · *Number 99* · *Sharp North*

## Pauline Chandler      Historical

Sally Gardner      Kate Pennington
Frances Mary Hendry      Alison Prince
Carolyn Meyer      Maggie Prince

*Warrior Girl*

## Gennifer Choldenko      Family  Social issues

Frank Cottrell Boyce      Linda Newbery
Eoin Colfer      Louis Sachar
Mark Haddon      Jerry Spinelli

*Al Capone Does My Shirts*

## Julia Clarke — Family   Social issues

Anne Fine     Sue Mayfield

*Between You and Me · Chasing Rainbows*
*The Other Alice · You Lose Some, You Win Some*

## Ann Coburn — Fantasy   Magic

Alison Croggon     Christopher Paolini
Marianne Curley     Kate Thompson
Margaret Mahy

*Flying Solo · Glint · Showtime*

## Stephen Cole — Horror   Science fiction   Thriller

Holly Black     Cate Tiernan
Darren Shan     Chris Wooding

*Thieves Like Us*
*Dr Who Series · The Wereling Trilogy*

## Eoin Colfer — Detective mysteries   Fantasy   Thrillers

Gennifer Choldenko     Terry Pratchett     8-11
Sally Gardner     J K Rowling
Mark Haddon     David Lee Stone
Anthony Horowitz     Rick Yancey

*Half Moon Investigations · The Supernaturalist · The Wish List*
*Artemis Fowl Series*

## Louise Cooper — Fantasy   Science fiction

Joan Aiken     Lesley Howarth     8-11
Aubrey Flegg

*Demon Crossing · Merrow*
*Mirror, Mirror Series*

## Susan Cooper — Adventure   Fantasy

Catherine Fisher     Cliff McNish     8-11
Charlie Fletcher     Tamora Pierce
Victoria Hanley     Katherine Roberts
Robin Jarvis     J R R Tolkien
Ursula Le Guin

*King of Shadows*
*The Dark is Rising Series*

## Joe Craig 💬
Adventure Thrillers

Charlie Higson
Sam Hutton
Andy McNab and Robert Rigby

Robert Muchamore
Malcolm Rose
Chris Ryan

*Jimmy Coates Series*

## Sharon Creech 💬
Adventure Diaries Family

Lynne Reid Banks
Theresa Breslin
Gillian Cross
Jennifer Donnelly
Michelle Magorian

Meg Rosoff
Louis Sachar
Nicky Singer
Jerry Spinelli
Karen Wallace

8-11

*Ruby Holler • Walk Two Moons • The Wanderer*

## Alison Croggon
Fantasy

Lloyd Alexander
Holly Black
N M Browne
Trudi Canavan
Ann Coburn

Marianne Curley
Katherine Roberts
G P Taylor
Catherine Webb

*The Pellinor Trilogy*

## Michael Cronin
War 1939-45

Martin Booth
John Boyne
Theresa Breslin
Carlo Gebler

Michael Morpurgo
James Riordan
Robert Westall
Markus Zusak

*Against the Day • In the Morning • Through the Night*

## Gillian Cross 💬
Adventure School Social issues Thrillers

Tim Bowler
Patrick Cave
Sharon Creech
Philip Gross
Brian Keaney

Geraldine McCaughrean
Jan Mark
Bali Rai
Jean Ure
Matt Whyman

8-11

*Calling a Dead Man • Tightrope*
*Dark Ground Series*

12-14

99

## Kevin Crossley-Holland 💬    Historical: Medieval   Mythology

N M Browne
Geraldine McCaughrean

Susan Price

8-11

*Gatty's Tale*
*Arthur Series*

## Marianne Curley          Fantasy   Magic

Holly Black
N M Browne
Trudi Canavan
Ann Coburn
Alison Croggon

Catherine Fisher
Katherine Roberts
Jonathan Stroud
Catherine Webb
Matt Whyman

*Guardians of Time Trilogy*

## Joseph Delaney 💬    Ghost/supernatural   Magic

Charlie Fletcher
Robin Jarvis
Diana Wynne Jones
Erik L'Homme
Marcus Sedgwick

Jonathan Stroud
J R R Tolkien
Chris Wooding
Rick Yancey

8-11

*The Spook's Apprentice* · *The Spook's Curse* · *The Spook's Secret*

## Narinder Dhami 💬    Family   Social issues   Sport

Anne Fine
Cathy Hopkins
Hilary McKay

Bali Rai
Jacqueline Wilson

8-11

*Bend It Like Beckham* · *Bhangra Babes*
*Bindi Babes* · *Bollywood Babes* · *Grow Up Dad!*

## John Dickinson 💬          Fantasy

Peter Dickinson
Stuart Hill
Hervé Jubert

Susan Price
Marcus Sedgwick
Kate Thompson

*The Cup of the World* · *The Widow and the King*

> Go to the back for lists of:
> Authors by Genre · Graphic novels · Prize winners · Exploring further

## Peter Dickinson 🗩

Adventure Fantasy Ghost/supernatural Social issues

John Dickinson
Susan Gates
Geraldine McCaughrean
Anthony Masters

Michelle Paver
Sally Prue
Kate Thompson
Robert Westall

*Angel Isle • The Gift Boat • The Ropemaker • Tears of the Salamander
The Changes Trilogy • The Kin Series*

## Berlie Doherty

Family Historical Social issues

8-11

Bernard Ashley
Theresa Breslin
Adèle Geras
Sandra Glover
Julia Green

Mary Hooper
Brian Keaney
Geraldine McCaughrean
Hilary McKay

*Dear Nobody • Deep Secret*

## Jennifer Donnelly

Historical Romance

Sharon Creech
Linda Newbery
Meg Rosoff

Mildred D Taylor
Karen Wallace

*A Gathering Light*

## Paul Dowswell

Adventure Historical: Victorian Sea/boats

Elizabeth Laird
Michael Molloy

Alison Prince

8-11

*The Adventures of Sam Witchall*

## Stephen Elboz

Fantasy Magic

Diana Wynne Jones
Ursula Le Guin
Cliff McNish

Maggie Prince
J K Rowling
J R R Tolkien

8-11

*A Land Without Magic • Ocean of Magic
A Store of Secrets [originally published as The Byzantium Bazaar]
The Tower at Moonville • A Wild Kind of Magic*

🗩 Some titles available as **Talking books**

**12-14**

101

## Deborah Ellis — Family Other cultures Other lands War

Nancy Farmer
Aubrey Flegg
Frances Mary Hendry
Gaye Hiçyilmaz

Adeline Yen Mah
Henning Mankell
Beverley Naidoo
Suzanne Fisher Staples

*The Breadwinner • The Heaven Shop • Mud City • Parvana's Journey*

12-14

## Nancy Farmer — Historical Mythology Other cultures

Deborah Ellis
Gaye Hiçyilmaz

Beverley Naidoo

*The House of the Scorpion • The Sea of Trolls*

## Josephine Feeney — Family School

Ros Asquith
Hilary McKay
Helena Pielichaty

Louise Rennison
Rosie Rushton

*The Dadhunters • Makeover Madness
So You Want to be the Perfect Family?*

## Anne Fine 💬 — Family Humour School Social issues

5-7 8-11

Veronica Bennett
Julie Bertagna
Frank Cottrell Boyce
Julia Clarke
Narinder Dhami

Catherine Forde
Helena Pielichaty
Alex Shearer
Jeremy Strong
Jacqueline Wilson

*Flour Babies • The Road of Bones • The Tulip Touch • Up on Cloud Nine*

## Catherine Fisher — Fantasy Horror Thrillers

8-11

N M Browne
Susan Cooper
Marianne Curley
Nick Gifford
Stuart Hill

Robin Jarvis
Diana Wynne Jones
Michael Lawrence
Ursula Le Guin
Catherine Webb

*Corbenic • Darkhenge • Darkwater Hall • The Lammas Field
The Book of the Crow Series*

## Aubrey Flegg
Historical  Other cultures  Social issues  War 1939-45

Louise Cooper
Deborah Ellis

Elizabeth Laird
Henning Mankell

*The Cinnamon Tree*
*The Louise Trilogy*

## Charlie Fletcher 💬
Adventure  Fantasy  Friends

Susan Cooper
Joseph Delaney

Robert Westall

8-11

*Stone Heart*

## Catherine Forde 💬
Friends  Social issues  Thrillers

Tim Bowler
Kevin Brooks
Anne Cassidy
Anne Fine

Keith Gray
Catherine MacPhail
Catherine Robinson
Benjamin Zephaniah

*The Drowning Pond* · *Exit Oz* BS
*Fat Boy Swim* · *Firestarter* · *L-L-L-Loser* BS · *Skarrs*

## Graham Gardner 💬
School  Social issues

Alan Gibbons

Pete Johnson

5-7 8-11

*Inventing Elliot*

## Sally Gardner 💬
Historical: 17th Century  Magic

Holly Black
Pauline Chandler
Eoin Colfer
Susan Gates

Mary Hoffman
Mary Hooper
Margaret Mahy
Ann Turnbull

8-11

*I, Coriander*

## Susan Gates 💬 Fantasy Historical Other cultures Science fiction

Melvin Burgess
Peter Dickinson
Sally Gardner

Margaret Mahy
Anthony Masters

8-11

*Cry Wolf* · *Dusk* · *Firebird*

> BS = Published by Barrington Stoke
> specialists in resources for dyslexic and struggling readers

12-14

103

## Jamila Gavin 🗩     Friends Historical Other cultures

Adèle Geras
Gaye Hiçyilmaz

Nicola Morgan
Suzanne Fisher Staples

5-7 8-11

*Coram Boy* · *The Wheel of Surya*

## Carlo Gebler     Fantasy Historical Mythology War 1939-45

Michael Cronin
Joan Lingard
Michael Morpurgo

James Riordan
Jerry Spinelli

*August '44* · *The Bull Raid* · *Caught on a Train*

## Adèle Geras 🗩     Fairy/folk Family Historical School

Julie Bertagna
Theresa Breslin
Berlie Doherty
Jamila Gavin
Shannon Hale

Hope Larson
Geraldine McCaughrean
Joan O'Neill
Theresa Tomlinson
Ann Turnbull

5-7 8-11

*Happy Ever After* · *Ithaka* · *Other Echoes* · *Troy*

## Alan Gibbons 🗩     Family Fantasy Social issues

Alison Allen-Gray
Sherry Ashworth
Kevin Brooks
Graham Gardner
Joan Lingard

Mal Peet
Bali Rai
Alex Shearer
Matt Whyman
Benjamin Zephaniah

8-11

*Blood Pressure* · *Caught in the Crossfire*
*Lost Boy's Appreciation Society* · *The Night Hunger* BS
*Rise of the Blood Moon* · *Setting of a Cruel Sun*

## Nick Gifford     Horror Thrillers

Catherine Fisher
Anthony Masters

Darren Shan
Cate Tiernan

*Erased* · *Flesh and Blood* · *Incubus* · *Piggies*

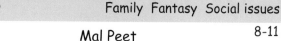

🗩 Some titles available as **Talking books**

## Morris Gleitzman  💬  Family  Humour  Social issues  War 1939-45

8-11

John Boyne
Matt Groening
Carl Hiaasen
Paul Jennings
Louis Sachar

Jeff Smith
Jerry Spinelli
Jeremy Strong
Sue Townsend
Markus Zusak

*Adults Only* · *Once* · *Worm Story*

## Sandra Glover  Friends  Ghost/supernatural  Social issues

8-11

David Almond
Rachel Anderson

Berlie Doherty
Jacqueline Wilson

*It Didn't Happen* · *Spiked*

## Keith Gray  Friends  Social issues

Kevin Brooks
Melvin Burgess
Catherine Forde

Pete Johnson
John Singleton
Robert Swindells

*Before Night Falls* BS · *The Chain* BS · *The Fearful* · *Malarkey*

## Julia Green  Social issues

Julie Bertagna
Berlie Doherty

Mary Hooper
Jan Mark

*Baby Blue* · *Blue Moon* · *Hunter's Heart*

## Matt Groening  Environment  Family  Humour  Science fiction

Morris Gleitzman
Terry Pratchett
Jeff Smith

Jeremy Strong
Marc Sumerak
Sue Townsend

*Futurama* GN · *The Simpsons* GN

## Philip Gross  Other cultures  Thrillers

Sherry Ashworth
Patrick Cave
Gillian Cross

Catherine MacPhail
Malcolm Rose

*Going For Stone* · *The Lastling* · *The Storm Garden*

GN = Graphic Novel

**12-14**

## Mark Haddon 💬     Crime Disability Family Social issues

Frank Cottrell Boyce       Eoin Colfer          8-11
Anne Cassidy               Anthony McGowan
Gennifer Choldenko

*The Curious Incident of the Dog in the Night-time*

## Ann Halam 💬            Ghost/supernatural Horror

Joan Aiken              E E Richardson
Rachel Anderson       John Singleton
Margaret Mahy         Chris Wooding
Celia Rees

*Finders Keepers* BS • *The Shadow on the Stairs* BS
*Siberia* • *Taylor Five* • *The Visitor*

## Shannon Hale                 Fantasy War

Adèle Geras         Theresa Tomlinson

*Enna Burning* • *The Goose Girl* • *River Secrets*

## Victoria Hanley 💬              Fantasy

Susan Cooper         Tanith Lee
Ursula Le Guin       Tamora Pierce
*The Healer's Keep* • *The Light of the Oracle* • *The Seer and the Sword*

## Frances Hardinge 💬          Fantasy

Joan Aiken           Mathew Skelton
Diana Wynne Jones

*Fly By Night*

## Sonya Hartnett             Social issues

David Almond         Philip Pullman
Tim Bowler           Mildred D Taylor
Kevin Brooks

*Stripes of the Sidestep Wolf* • *Surrender* • *Thursday's Child*

## Julie Hearn 💬    Ghost/supernatural Historical Social issues

Andrew Matthews     Maggie Prince
Michael Molloy         Celia Rees

*Follow Me Down* • *The Merrybegot*

## Lian Hearn

Fantasy Historical Other cultures

Melvin Burgess
William Nicholson
Garth Nix

Susan Price
Philip Reeve
Beth Webb

*Tales of the Otori*

## Frances Mary Hendry

Ballet Historical: Roman

Rachel Anderson
Pauline Chandler

Deborah Ellis
Elizabeth Laird

*Angel Dancer* BS
*Gladiatrix Series*

12-14

## Carl Hiaasen

Environment Family Humour Social issues

Morris Gleitzman
Louis Sachar

Jerry Spinelli

*Flush · Hoot*

## Gaye Hiçyilmaz

Family Other cultures Social issues

Deborah Ellis
Nancy Farmer
Jamila Gavin
Elizabeth Laird
Joan Lingard

Beverley Naidoo
Suzanne Fisher Staples
Robert Swindells
Benjamin Zephaniah

*Coming Home · Girl in Red · Pictures from the Fire*

## Charlie Higson

Adventure

Dominic Barker
David Belbin
A J Butcher
Joe Craig
Anthony Horowitz

Sam Hutton
Andy McNab and Robert Rigby
Robert Muchamore
M E Rabb
Chris Ryan

8-11

*Young Bond Series*

## Stuart Hill

Fantasy

John Dickinson
Catherine Fisher
William Nicholson

Garth Nix
Michelle Paver
J R R Tolkien

*Chronicles of Icemark*

## Nigel Hinton — Adventure Family Fantasy Thrillers

Veronica Bennett
S E Hinton
Pete Johnson

Graham Marks
Louis Sachar

8-11

*Until Proven Guilty* BS
*The Buddy Series*

## S E Hinton  — Social issues

Melvin Burgess
Nigel Hinton

Pete Johnson
Catherine MacPhail

*The Outsiders* · *Rumblefish*

## Mary Hoffman — Adventure Family Fantasy Historical

Sally Gardner
Eva Ibbotson
Diana Wynne Jones

Kai Meyer
Donna Jo Napoli

5-7

*Stravaganza Series*

## Mary Hooper  — Family Friends Historical Social issues

Kate Cann
Berlie Doherty
Sally Gardner
Julia Green
Cathy Hopkins

Eva Ibbotson
Karen McCombie
Tom Pow
Dyan Sheldon
Ann Turnbull

5-7 8-11

*Amy* · *At the Sign of the Sugared Plum* · *Petals From the Ashes*
*The Remarkable Life and Times of Eliza Rose* · *Zara*

## Cathy Hopkins  — Family Humour Romance Social issues

Ann Brashares
Meg Cabot
Kate Cann
Narinder Dhami
Mary Hooper

Kathryn Lamb
Sue Limb
Karen McCombie
Louise Rennison
Dyan Sheldon

*Mates Dates Series* · *Truth, Dare, Kiss or Promise Series*

Go to the back for lists of:
Authors by Genre · Graphic novels · Prize winners · Exploring further

## Anthony Horowitz 💬 Adventure Horror Humour Thrillers

8-11

David Belbin
A J Butcher
Eoin Colfer
Charlie Higson
Sam Hutton

Andy McNab and Robert Rigby
Robert Muchamore
Chris Ryan
Nick Shadow
Eleanor Updale

*Stormbreaker* GN
*Alex Rider Series* · *Power of Five Series*

12-14

## Lesley Howarth 💬 Environment Family Thrillers

8-11

Julie Bertagna
Louise Cooper
Rhiannon Lassiter

Jan Mark
William Nicholson
Celia Rees

*Calling the Shots* · *Carwash* · *Colossus*
*Dade County's Big Summer* BS · *Ultraviolet*

## Sam Hutton Adventure Crime Detective mysteries Thrillers

David Belbin
A J Butcher
Joe Craig
Charlie Higson
Anthony Horowitz

Andy McNab and Robert Rigby
Robert Muchamore
Malcolm Rose
Chris Ryan

*Special Agents Series*

## Eva Ibbotson 💬 Adventure Ghost/supernatural Humour

8-11

Frank Cottrell Boyce
Mary Hoffman

Mary Hooper
Karen Wallace

*Journey to the River Sea* · *The Star of Kazan* · *Which Witch*

## Brian Jacques 💬 Adventure Fantasy

8-11

Robin Jarvis
Terry Pratchett
Jonathan Stroud

J R R Tolkien
Clive Woodall

*Flying Dutchman Series* · *Redwall Series*

💬 Some titles available as **Talking books**

## Robin Jarvis 💬

Fantasy

8-11

Joan Aiken
Susan Cooper
Joseph Delaney
Catherine Fisher

Brian Jacques
Terry Pratchett
Jonathan Stroud
Chris Wooding

*Intrigues of the Reflected Realm Series*
*Tales From the Wyrd Museum Series* · *Whitby Witches Series*

12-14

## Ben Jeapes

Historical  Science fiction  Thrillers

Joan Aiken
Jan Mark

William Nicholson
Philip Pullman

*The New World Order* · *The Winged Chariot* · *The Xenocide Mission*

## Paul Jennings 💬

Ghost/supernatural  Humour  Thrillers

Frank Cottrell Boyce
Morris Gleitzman

Pete Johnson
Jeremy Strong

8-11

*How Hedley Hopkins did a Dare, ...*
*Tongue-tied* · *Unseen*

## Pete Johnson

Fantasy  Ghost/supernatural  Romance  Social issues

Veronica Bennett
Terence Blacker
Graham Gardner
Keith Gray
Nigel Hinton

S E Hinton
Paul Jennings
Louis Sachar
John Singleton
Jeremy Strong

8-11

*Diary of an Unteenager* BS · *The Ex-files*
*Faking It* · *The Hero Game* · *How Embarassing is That*

## Diana Wynne Jones 💬

Fantasy

8-11

Joan Aiken
Joseph Delaney
Stephen Elboz
Catherine Fisher
Frances Hardinge

Mary Hoffman
Michael Lawrence
Ursula Le Guin
J K Rowling
Catherine Webb

*The Merlin Conspiracy* · *Power of Three*
*Chrestomanci Series*

## Hervé Jubert
Crime  Detective mysteries  Fantasy  Thrillers

John Dickinson
Philip Reeve

Marcus Sedgwick
Jonathan Stroud

*Dance of the Assassins* · *Devil's Tango*

## Susan Juby
Humour  Romance  Social issues

Raffaella Barker
Sue Limb
Louise Rennison

Dyan Sheldon
Sue Townsend

*I'm Alice (Beauty Queen)* · *I'm Alice (I Think?)*

## Brian Keaney
Death  Family  Social issues

Veronica Bennett
Tim Bowler
Gillian Cross

Berlie Doherty
Valerie Mendes
Linda Newbery

*Jacob's Ladder* · *No Stone Unturned* BS · *Where Mermaids Sing*

## Penny Kendal
Thrillers

David Belbin
Melvin Burgess

Catherine MacPhail
Robert Swindells

*Broken* · *Christina's Face* · *Keeping Quiet*

## Erik L'Homme
Horror  Magic

Joseph Delaney

Anthony Masters

*Book of the Stars Series*

## Elizabeth Laird
Adventure  Family  Other cultures  Social issues

Lynne Reid Banks
Paul Dowswell
Aubrey Flegg
Frances Mary Hendry
Gaye Hiçyilmaz

Adeline Yen Mah
Michael Molloy
Beverley Naidoo
Donna Jo Napoli
Suzanne Fisher Staples

8-11

*The Garbage King* · *Jake's Tower* · *A Little Piece of Ground*
*Oranges in No Man's Land* · *Paradise End* · *Secrets of the Fearless*

BS = Published by Barrington Stoke
specialists in resources for dyslexic and struggling readers

12-14

## Kathryn Lamb

Ros Asquith
Meg Cabot
Cathy Cassidy
Cathy Hopkins
Sue Limb

Karen McCombie
Caroline Plaisted
Louise Rennison
Rosie Rushton

*Honestly Mum*
*Alex Series* · *Best Mates Forever Series*

**12-14**

## Hope Larson
Fantasy  Magic  Pony/horse

Raffaella Barker
Adèle Geras

Ted Naifeh

*Gray Horses* GN · *Salamander Dream* GN

## Rhiannon Lassiter
Computers  Fantasy  Science fiction

Lesley Howarth
Tamora Pierce
Chloë Rayban

Katherine Roberts
Catherine Webb

*Waking Dream*
*Hex Series* · *Rights of Passage Series*

## Michael Lawrence
Fantasy

Catherine Fisher
Diana Wynne Jones
Tamora Pierce

Susan Price
Alex Shearer

8-11

*Aldous Lexicon Series*

## Ursula Le Guin 💬
Fantasy  Magic

Susan Cooper
Stephen Elboz
Catherine Fisher
Victoria Hanley
Diana Wynne Jones

Garth Nix
Tamora Pierce
J R R Tolkien
Beth Webb
Scott Westerfield

*Gifts* · *Voices*
*The Earthsea Series*

💬 Some titles available as **Talking books**

## Tanith Lee

Victoria Hanley
Joshua Mowll
Ted Naifeh

Tamora Pierce
Celia Rees

*Piratica · Piratica II*
*The Claidi Journals*

## Sue Limb

Friends  Humour

Ros Asquith
Cathy Cassidy
Cathy Hopkins
Susan Juby

Kathryn Lamb
Karen McCombie
Louise Rennison

*Girl 15: Charming But Insane · Girl Nearly 16: Absolute Torture*
*Ruby Rogers is a Waste of Space*

## Joan Lingard

Social issues  War

5-7

Lynne Reid Banks
Theresa Breslin
Carlo Gebler
Alan Gibbons

Gaye Hiçyilmaz
Linda Newbery
Benjamin Zephaniah

*Kevin and Sadie Series · Maggie Series*

## Geraldine McCaughrean

Family  Fantasy
Historical  Other cultures

5-7 8-11

Gillian Cross
Kevin Crossley-Holland
Peter Dickinson
Berlie Doherty
Adèle Geras

Sally Prue
Theresa Tomlinson
Eleanor Updale
Jeanette Winterson

*Cyrano · The Kite Rider · The White Darkness*

## Karen McCombie

Family  Friends  Humour  Social issues

8-11

Ros Asquith
Ann Brashares
Kate Cann
Mary Hooper

Cathy Hopkins
Kathryn Lamb
Sue Limb
Natsuki Takaya

*Sisters · Marshmallow Magic and the Wild Rose Rouge*
*Ally's World Series · Stella Etc Series*

12-14

## Anthony McGowan    Death  Humour  Illness  Social issues

Kevin Brooks                    Mark Haddon

*Henry Tumour*

## Hilary McKay 🗨    Family  Humour  Social issues

Cathy Cassidy            Josephine Feeney        5-7 8-11
Narinder Dhami           Rosie Rushton
Berlie Doherty

*Caddy Ever After* · *Indigo's Star* · *Permanent Rose* · *Saffy's Angel*
*The Exiles*

## Andy McNab and Robert Rigby 🗨    Adventure  Thrillers

A J Butcher              Sam Hutton
Joe Craig                Robert Muchamore
Charlie Higson           Chris Ryan
Anthony Horowitz

*Avenger* · *Boy Soldier* · *Payback*

## Cliff McNish    Fantasy  Ghost/supernatural  Magic

Susan Cooper             Michelle Paver
Stephen Elboz            J K Rowling
William Nicholson

*Breathe: A Ghost Story*
*The Doomspell Trilogy* · *Silver Sequence*

## Catherine MacPhail    Adventure  Disability  Fantasy  Social issues

Bernard Ashley           S E Hinton              8-11
Julie Bertagna           Penny Kendal
Catherine Forde          Graham Marks
Philip Gross             Robert Swindells

*Another Me* · *Dark Waters* · *Fighting Back*
*A Kind of Magic* BS · *Roxy's Baby* · *Underworld*

Go to the back for
lists of:
Authors by Genre
Graphic novels
Prize winners
Further reading

## Michelle Magorian 💬     Family   War 1939-45

8-11

Rachel Anderson
Theresa Breslin
Sharon Creech
Joan O'Neill

Mal Peet
K M Peyton
James Riordan

*Goodnight Mister Tom • A Little Love Song • A Spoonful of Jam*

## Adeline Yen Mah 💬    Family   Other cultures   War 1939-45

Deborah Ellis
Elizabeth Laird
Beverley Naidoo

Donna Jo Napoli
Jacqueline Wilson

*Chinese Cinderella • Chinese Cinderella and the Secret Dragon Society*

## Margaret Mahy        Fantasy   Social issues

8-11

Ann Coburn
Sally Gardner

Susan Gates
Ann Halam

*Alchemy • The Changeover • Maddigan's Fantasia*

## Henning Mankell        Other cultures   Social issues

Deborah Ellis
Aubrey Flegg

Beverley Naidoo

*A Bridge to the Stars • Playing with Fire*

## Jan Mark     Family   Fantasy   Historical: Tudor   Social issues

8-11

Bernard Ashley
Gillian Cross
Julia Green
Lesley Howarth
Ben Jeapes

Mal Peet
Tom Pow
Alison Prince
Sally Prue
Matt Whyman

*The Electric Telepath • Riding Tycho
Something in the Air • Stratford Boys • Turbulence • Voyager*

## Graham Marks     Family   Historical: Victorian   Social issues   Thrillers

Tim Bowler
Nigel Hinton

Catherine MacPhail
Matt Whyman

*How it Works • Radio Radio
Snatched! • Tokyo: All Alone in The Big City • Zoo*

12-14

## Anthony Masters 💬

Adventure Ghost/supernatural
Horror Thrillers
5-7 8-11

Peter Dickinson
Susan Gates
Nick Gifford
Erik L'Homme
E E Richardson

Malcolm Rose
Nick Shadow
R L Stine
Robert Westall

*The Drop · Stalker* BS *· Web of Terror*

## Andrew Matthews

Fantasy Friends Ghost/supernatural
War 1914-18

Meg Cabot
Julie Hearn
Michael Morpurgo
K M Peyton

Celia Rees
Cate Tiernan
Jennie Walters

*From Above, with Love · The Swallow and the Dark*

## Sue Mayfield

Friends Social issues

Sherry Ashworth
Julia Clarke

Dyan Sheldon

*Poisoned · Voices*

## Valerie Mendes

Death Family

Tim Bowler
Brian Keaney

Linda Newbery

*Coming of Age · The Drowning · Lost and Found*

## Carolyn Meyer 💬

Diaries Historical: Tudor

Pauline Chandler
Kate Pennington

Maggie Prince

*Beware Princess Elizabeth · Mary Bloody Mary*

## Kai Meyer 💬

Fantasy Other cultures

Mary Hoffman

Philip Reeve

*The Flowing Queen · Stone Light*

BS = Published by Barrington Stoke
specialists in resources for dyslexic and struggling readers

## Michael Molloy

Adventure  Historical: Victorian

Paul Dowswell
Julie Hearn

Elizabeth Laird

8-11

*Peter Raven Under Fire*

## Nicola Morgan

Death  Fantasy  Historical  Social issues

David Almond
David Belbin
Jamila Gavin

Tom Pow
Ann Turnbull

*Chicken Friend* · *Fleshmarket*
*The Highwayman's Footsteps* · *Mondays are Red* · *Sleepwalking*

## Michael Morpurgo ⌐

Animals  Historical  War 1939-45

Rachel Anderson
Martin Booth
John Boyne
Michael Cronin
Carlo Gebler

Andrew Matthews
Mal Peet
James Riordan
Robert Westall
Markus Zusak

5-7 8-11

*Out of the Ashes* · *Out on the Wide Wide Sea* · *Private Peaceful*

## Joshua Mowll

Adventure  Family  Fantasy  Other cultures

Tanith Lee
Philip Pullman

Marcus Sedgwick

8-11

*Operation Red Jericho* · *Operation Typhoon Shore*

## Robert Muchamore

Adventure  Friends  Thrillers

A J Butcher
Joe Craig
Charlie Higson
Anthony Horowitz
Sam Hutton

Andy McNab and Robert Rigby
M E Rabb
Malcolm Rose
Chris Ryan
Marc Sumerak

*CHERUB Series*

> Go to back for
> lists of:
> Authors by Genre
> Graphic novels
> Prize winners
> Further reading

**12-14**

## Beverley Naidoo 💬     Other lands   Social issues

Lynne Reid Banks
Deborah Ellis
Nancy Farmer
Gaye Hiçyilmaz
Elizabeth Laird

Adeline Yen Mah
Henning Mankell
Donna Jo Napoli
Benjamin Zephaniah

*Journey to Jo'burg* · *The Other Side of Truth*
*Out of Bounds* · *Web of Lies*

**12-14**

## Ted Naifeh     Fantasy   Magic

Hope Larson
Tanith Lee
Terry Pratchett

J K Rowling
Natsuki Takaya

*Polly and the Pirates* GN
*Courtney Cumrin Series* GN

## Donna Jo Napoli     Historical   Other cultures   War 1939-45

Mary Hoffman
Elizabeth Laird

Adeline Yen Mah
Beverley Naidoo

*Daughter of Venice* · *Stones in Water*

## Linda Newbery     Family   Illness   Social issues   War 1914-18

8-11

Rachel Anderson
Martin Booth
Gennifer Choldenko
Jennifer Donnelly
Brian Keaney

Joan Lingard
Valerie Mendes
K M Peyton
Ann Turnbull
Robert Westall

*Set in Stone* · *The Shell House* · *Sisterland*
*Moving On Trilogy* · *Shouting Wind Trilogy*

## William Nicholson 💬     Adventure   Fantasy

8-11

Stephen Bowkett
Lian Hearn
Stuart Hill
Lesley Howarth
Ben Jeapes

Cliff McNish
Susan Price
Sally Prue
Philip Reeve
J K Rowling

*Seeker* · *Web of Lies*
*Wind On Fire Trilogy*

## Garth Nix ✐

Adventure  Fantasy

Lloyd Alexander
Trudi Canavan
Marianne Curley
Lian Hearn
Stuart Hill

Ursula Le Guin
Christopher Paolini
Beth Webb
Scott Westerfield
Chris Wooding

*The Ragwitch* • *Shade's Children*
*Keys to the Kingdom Series* • *Old Kingdom Series*

## Joan O'Neill

Historical  Social issues  War 1939-45

Joan Bauer
Ann Brashares
Theresa Breslin

Adèle Geras
Michelle Magorian
Alison Prince

*Dream Chaser*
*Daisy Chain War Trilogy*

## Christopher Paolini ✐

Fantasy

Trudi Canavan
Ann Coburn
Garth Nix
Philip Reeve

Marcus Sedgwick
Mathew Skelton
Dugald Steer

*Eldest* • *Eragon*

## James Patterson

Friends  Science fiction  Social issues

Alison Allen-Gray
Malcolm Rose

Marc Sumerak

*Maximum Ride Series*

## Michelle Paver ✐

Fantasy

8-11

Peter Dickinson
Stuart Hill
Cliff McNish
Susan Price

J K Rowling
J R R Tolkien
Beth Webb

*Soul Eater* • *Spirit Walker* • *Wolf Brother*

GN = Graphic Novel

## Mal Peet
Mystery  Social issues  Sport

Alan Gibbons
Michelle Magorian
Jan Mark

Michael Morpurgo
James Riordan
Matt Whyman

*Keeper* · *The Penalty* · *Tamar*

## Kate Pennington
Historical: Tudor, Victorian  Mystery

Pauline Chandler
Carolyn Meyer

Alison Prince
Maggie Prince

*Brief Candle* · *Charley Feather* · *Nightingales Song* · *Tread Softly*

## K M Peyton
Historical  Pony/horse  Social issues

Michelle Magorian
Andrew Matthews

Linda Newbery
Jennie Walters

*Greater Gains* · *Small Gains*

## Helena Pielichaty
Family  Social issues

8-11

Malorie Blackman
Josephine Feeney
Anne Fine

Bali Rai
Jacqueline Wilson

*Getting Rid of Karenna* · *Jade's Story* · *Never Ever*
*Simone Series*

## Tamora Pierce
Fantasy  Magic

Holly Black
Trudi Canavan
Susan Cooper
Victoria Hanley
Rhiannon Lassiter

Michael Lawrence
Ursula Le Guin
Tanith Lee
Susan Price
Katherine Roberts

*Trickster's Choice*
*Circle of Magic Quartet* · *The Circle Opens Quartet* · *The Immortals Quartet*
*The Protector of the Small Quartet* · *Song of the Lioness Series*

GN = Graphic Novel
BS = Published by Barrington Stoke
specialists in resources for dyslexic and struggling readers

12-14

## Caroline Plaisted
**Family Humour**

8-11

Ros Asquith
Kathryn Lamb
Chloë Rayban

Rosie Rushton
Jean Ure

*10 Things to Do Before You're 16 · 10 Ways to Cope With Boys*
*Cringe · Living With a Reinvented Mum*
*No Way Am I Living With Her · Reinventing Mum*

## Tom Pow
**Mystery Science fiction**

12-14

Tim Bowler
Mary Hooper
Jan Mark
Nicola Morgan

Alison Prince
Eleanor Updale
Lee Weatherly

*Captives · The Pack · Scabbit Isle*

## Terry Pratchett 
**Fantasy Humour**

8-11

Eoin Colfer
Matt Groening
Brian Jacques
Robin Jarvis

Ted Naifeh
David Lee Stone
Jonathan Stroud

*Guards, Guards* BS · *A Hat Full of Sky*
*Mort* GN · *Wee Free Men · Wintersmith*
*Bromeliad Trilogy · The Discworld Series · Johnny Maxwell Stories*

## Susan Price
**Fantasy Ghost/supernatural**
**Mythology Science fiction**

8-11

David Almond
Kevin Crossley-Holland
John Dickinson
Lian Hearn
Michael Lawrence

William Nicholson
Michelle Paver
Tamora Pierce
Sally Prue
Celia Rees

*Odin's Queen · Odin's Voice*
*The Sterkarm Handshake · A Sterkarm Kiss · The Wolf Sisters*

## Alison Prince
**Family Historical: Victorian War 1939-45**

Rachel Anderson
Pauline Chandler
Paul Dowswell
Jan Mark
Joan O'Neill

Kate Pennington
Tom Pow
Maggie Prince
Mildred D Taylor

*Doodlebug Summer · Jacoby's Game · Luck* BS · *Smoke* BS

## Maggie Prince
Historical  Magic

Pauline Chandler
Stephen Elboz
Julie Hearn
Carolyn Meyer

Kate Pennington
Alison Prince
Celia Rees

*North Side of the Tree  ·  Raider's Tide*

12-14

## Sally Prue ⌒
Fantasy  Humour  Social issues

Peter Dickinson
Jan Mark
Geraldine McCaughrean

William Nicholson
Susan Price
Kate Thompson

*Cold Tom  ·  The Devil's Toenail  ·  Goldkeeper*
*James and the Alien Experiment  ·  Kaleidoscope  ·  Ryland's Footsteps*

## Philip Pullman ⌒
Fantasy  Historical: Victorian
Social issues  Thrillers
8-11

Sonya Hartnett
Ben Jeapes
Joshua Mowll
Philip Reeve
J K Rowling

Mathew Skelton
Kate Thompson
J R R Tolkien
Karen Wallace
Jeanette Winterson

*The Broken Bridge  ·  Buttefly Tattoo*
*His Dark Materials Trilogy  ·  Tiger in the Smoke Series*

## M E Rabb
Mystery  Thrillers

David Belbin
A J Butcher
Meg Cabot

Charlie Higson
Robert Muchamore

*Missing Persons Series*

## Bali Rai ⌒
Other cultures  School
8-11

Gillian Cross
Narinder Dhami
Alan Gibbons

Helena Pielichaty
Jacqueline Wilson

*Dream On  BS  ·  The Last Taboo  ·  Rani and Sukh*
*Two Timer  BS  ·  (Un)arranged Marriage  ·  The Whisper*
*Tales From Devana High*

## Chloë Rayban
Family Romance

Ros Asquith
Raffaella Barker
Malorie Blackman

Rhiannon Lassiter
Caroline Plaisted
Rosie Rushton

*Drama Queen* · *My Life Staring Mom* · *Wrong Number* BS

## Celia Rees 💬
Ghost/supernatural Historical
Social issues Thrillers

Julie Bertagna
Malorie Blackman
Ann Halam
Julie Hearn
Lesley Howarth

Tanith Lee
Andrew Matthews
Susan Price
Maggie Prince
Cate Tiernan

8-11

*City of Shadows* · *The Host Rides Out* · *Pirates!*
*Sorceress* · *The Soul Taker* · *The Wish House*

## Philip Reeve 💬
Fantasy

Stephen Bowkett
Lian Hearn
Hervé Jubert
Kai Meyer
William Nicholson

Christopher Paolini
Philip Pullman
Dugald Steer
Kate Thompson
Chris Wooding

8-11

*A Darkling Plain* · *Infernal Devices*
*Larklight* · *Mortal Engines* · *Predator's Gold*

## Louise Rennison 💬
Diaries Humour Romance

Ros Asquith
Meg Cabot
Josephine Feeney
Cathy Hopkins
Susan Juby

Kathryn Lamb
Sue Limb
Rosie Rushton
Dyan Sheldon
Sue Townsend

*Confessions of Georgia Nicholson*

## E E Richardson
Horror

Ann Halam
Anthony Masters

Darren Shan

*The Devil's Footsteps* · *The Intruders*

💬 Some titles available as **Talking books**

## James Riordan
Disability  Friends  Social issues

Martin Booth
Michael Cronin
Carlo Gebler
Michelle Magorian

Michael Morpurgo
Mal Peet
Robert Westall

*The Cello · The Gift*

12-14

## Katherine Roberts
Fantasy  Mythology

N M Browne
Trudi Canavan
Susan Cooper
Alison Croggon
Marianne Curley

Rhiannon Lassiter
Tamora Pierce
Dugald Steer
Catherine Webb
Rick Yancey

8-11

*Seven Fabulous Wonders Series*

## Catherine Robinson
Family  Friends  Romance  Social issues

Raffaella Barker
Joan Bauer

Ann Brashares
Catherine Forde

*Celia · Mr Perfect · Soul Sisters · Tin Grin*

## Malcolm Rose
Social issues  Thrillers

A J Butcher
Patrick Cave
Joe Craig
Philip Gross
Sam Hutton

Anthony Masters
Robert Muchamore
James Patterson
Robert Swindells

*Bloodline · Clone · The Death Gene*
*Hurricane Force · Transplant*
*Traces Series*

## Meg Rosoff ⌕
Adventure  Family  Social issues  War

Joan Bauer
Theresa Breslin
Anne Cassidy
Sharon Creech
Jennifer Donnelly

Mildred D Taylor
Robert Westall
Scott Westerfield
Jeanette Winterson

*How I Live Now · Just in Case*

# J K Rowling 💬

Fantasy Magic School

8-11

Eoin Colfer
Stephen Elboz
Diana Wynne Jones
Cliff McNish
Ted Naifeh

William Nicholson
Michelle Paver
Philip Pullman
Marcus Sedgwick
G P Taylor

*The Harry Potter Series*

# Rosie Rushton

Family Humour Letters Social issues

Sherry Ashworth
Cathy Cassidy
Josephine Feeney
Kathryn Lamb
Hilary McKay

Caroline Plaisted
Chloë Rayban
Louise Rennison
Dyan Sheldon
Lee Weatherly

*Fallout* BS · *Friends, Enemies and Other Tiny Problems*
*Jessica* · *The Secrets of Love*
*Tell Me I'm OK Really* · *Waving Not Drowning*
*What a Week ..... Series*

# Chris Ryan

Adventure Social issues Thrillers

A J Butcher
Joe Craig
Charlie Higson
Anthony Horowitz

Sam Hutton
Andy McNab and Robert Rigby
Robert Muchamore

*Flash Flood*
*Alpha Force Series*

# Louis Sachar 💬

Humour School Social issues

5-7 8-11

David Almond
Gennifer Choldenko
Sharon Creech
Morris Gleitzman
Carl Hiaasen

Nigel Hinton
Pete Johnson
Nicky Singer
Jerry Spinelli

*Holes* · *Small Steps*

BS = Published by Barrington Stoke
specialists in resources for dyslexic and struggling readers

125

# Marcus Sedgwick 💬

Environment  Ghost/supernatural
Historical  Mystery

David Almond
Joseph Delaney
John Dickinson
Hervé Jubert
Joshua Mowll

Christopher Paolini
J K Rowling
G P Taylor
Chris Wooding

*Book of Dead Days* · *The Dark Flight Down* · *The Dark Horse*
*The Foreshadowing* · *My Swordhand is Singing* · *Witch Hill*

# Nick Shadow

Horror

Anthony Horowitz
Anthony Masters

Darren Shan
R L Stine

8-11

*The Midnight Library*

# Darren Shan 💬

Horror

Stephen Cole
Nick Gifford
E E Richardson
Nick Shadow

R L Stine
Cate Tiernan
Chris Wooding

*Demonata Series* · *The Saga of Darren Shan*

# Alex Shearer 💬

Family  Science fiction  Social issues

Anne Fine
Alan Gibbons

Michael Lawrence
Jonathan Stroud

*Bootleg* · *The Great Blue Yonder* · *The Hunted*
*Lost* · *The Speed of the Dark* · *The Stolen*

# Dyan Sheldon 💬

Other cultures  Romance  School  Social issues

Mary Hooper
Cathy Hopkins
Susan Juby

Sue Mayfield
Louise Rennison
Rosie Rushton

5-7 8-11

*Confessions of a Holiday Star* · *Confessions of a Teenage Drama Queen*
*I Conquer Britain* · *My Perfect Life* · *Sophie Pitt-Turnbull Discovers America*

# Nicky Singer 💬

Detective mysteries  Ghost/supernatural
Social issues

Malorie Blackman
Kevin Brooks
Sharon Creech

Louis Sachar
Jerry Spinelli

*Doll* · *Feather Boy* · *The Innocent's Story*

## John Singleton
Family  Illness  Social issues

David Almond
Keith Gray

Ann Halam
Pete Johnson

*Angel Blood · Skinny B, Skaz and Me · Star*

## Mathew Skelton
Fantasy  Magic

Frances Hardinge
Christopher Paolini

Philip Pullman
Eleanor Updale

8-11

*Endymion Spring*

## Jeff Smith
Family  Humour

Morris Gleitzman
Matt Groening

Jeremy Strong

*The Crown of Horns* GN · *Ghost Circles* GN
*The Great Cow Race* GN · *Out From Boneville* GN

## Jerry Spinelli
Romance  School  Social issues  War 1939-45

John Boyne
Gennifer Choldenko
Sharon Creech
Carlo Gebler

Morris Gleitzman
Carl Hiaasen
Louis Sachar
Nicky Singer

*Milkweed · Stargirl*

## Suzanne Fisher Staples
Other cultures  Other lands

Lynne Reid Banks
John Boyne
Deborah Ellis
Jamila Gavin

Gaye Hiçyilmaz
Elizabeth Laird
Tim Wynne-Jones

*Shabanu: Daughter of the Wind*
*Shiva's Fire · Storm · Under the Persimmon Tree*

## Dugald Steer
Fantasy  Magic  Mythology

Christopher Paolini
Philip Reeve

Katherine Roberts
Karen Wallace

8-11

*Dragonology · Piratology · Wizardology*

12-14

GN = Graphic Novel

127

## R L Stine Horror

8-11

Anthony Masters
Nick Shadow

Darren Shan
Robert Westall

*Fear Street Series*

## David Lee Stone  Fantasy  Humour

8-11

Eoin Colfer

Terry Pratchett

*The Illmoor Chronicles*

**12-14**

## Jeremy Strong Humour  Social issues

5-7 8-11

Anne Fine
Morris Gleitzman
Matt Groening

Paul Jennings
Pete Johnson
Jeff Smith

*The Smallest Horse in the World* BS
*Stuff: The Life of a Cool Demented Dude*

## Jonathan Stroud  Fantasy  Social issues

Lloyd Alexander
Marianne Curley
Joseph Delaney
Brian Jacques
Robin Jarvis

Hervé Jubert
Terry Pratchett
Alex Shearer
G P Taylor
Chris Wooding

*Bartimaeus Trilogy*

## Marc Sumerak Family  School  Science fiction

Alison Allen-Gray
Matt Groening

Robert Muchamore
James Patterson

*Machine Teen*
*X-Men Powerpack Series* GN

## Robert Swindells Science fiction  Social issues  Thrillers  War

8-11

David Almond
Martin Booth
Anne Cassidy
Keith Gray
Gaye Hiçyilmaz

Penny Kendal
Catherine MacPhail
Malcolm Rose
Kate Thompson
Benjamin Zephaniah

*Branded · No Angels · Ruby Tanya*
*Snapshot* BS *· Stone Cold · Wrecked*

## Natsuki Takaya Adventure Friends

Karen McCombie

Ted Naifeh

*Fruits Basket Series* GN

## G P Taylor 💬 Adventure Fantasy Horror Magic

Trudi Canavan
Alison Croggon
J K Rowling

Marcus Sedgwick
Jonathan Stroud

*The Curse of Salamander Street*
*Shadowmancer* · *Tersias* · *Wormwood*

## Mildred D Taylor 💬 Historical Other lands

Malorie Blackman
Jennifer Donnelly
Sonya Hartnett

Alison Prince
Meg Rosoff

*Roll of Thunder, Hear My Cry*

## Kate Thompson 💬 Animals Fantasy Science fiction Social issues

Malorie Blackman
Ann Coburn
John Dickinson
Peter Dickinson

Sally Prue
Philip Pullman
Philip Reeve
Robert Swindells

8-11

*The Alchemist's Apprentice* · *Anan Water*
*The Beguilers* · *The Fourth Horseman* · *The New Policeman*
*The Missing Link Trilogy* · *The Switchers Trilogy*

## Cate Tiernan Magic

Stephen Cole
Nick Gifford
Andrew Matthews

Celia Rees
Darren Shan
Chris Wooding

*Wicca Series*

---

GN = Graphic Novel
BS = Published by Barrington Stoke
specialists in resources for dyslexic and struggling readers

## J R R Tolkien 💬 — Fantasy

8-11

Susan Cooper
Joseph Delaney
Stephen Elboz
Stuart Hill
Brian Jacques

Ursula Le Guin
Michelle Paver
Philip Pullman
Clive Woodall

*The Hobbit* GN · *The Lord of the Rings*

12-14

## Theresa Tomlinson — Family Historical

8-11

Adèle Geras
Geraldine McCaughrean

Shannon Hale

*The Moon Riders* · *The Voyage of the Snake Lady* · *The Wolf Girl*
*Forestwife Trilogy*

## Sue Townsend 💬 — Diaries Humour

Morris Gleitzman
Matt Groening
Susan Juby

Louise Rennison
Jacqueline Wilson

*Adrian Mole Series*

## Ann Turnbull — Historical Romance

Sally Gardner
Adèle Geras
Mary Hooper

Nicola Morgan
Linda Newbery

*Forged in the Fire* · *No Shame No Fear*

## Eleanor Updale 💬 — Crime Historical

Anthony Horowitz
Geraldine McCaughrean
Tom Pow

Mathew Skelton
Karen Wallace
Catherine Webb

*Montmorency Series*

## Jean Ure 💬 — Family Other cultures Romance Social issues

8-11

Ros Asquith
Cathy Cassidy

Gillian Cross
Caroline Plaisted

*Bad Alice* · *Get a Life!* · *A Twist in Time*

## Karen Wallace 💬   Adventure  Friends  Historical  Social issues

Veronica Bennett
Sharon Creech
Jennifer Donnelly
Eva Ibbotson

Philip Pullman
Dugald Steer
Eleanor Updale
Jennie Walters

5-7 8-11

*Climbing A Monkey Puzzle Tree · Raspberries on the Yangtze*
*The Unrivalled Spangles · Wendy*
*Lady Violet Winters Series*

## Jennie Walters                                    Historical: Victorian

Andrew Matthews
K M Peyton

Karen Wallace

8-11

*Swallowcliffe Hall*

## Lee Weatherly                                      Friends  Social issues

Anne Cassidy
Tom Pow

Rosie Rushton
Matt Whyman

*Breakfast at Sadie's · Child X*
*Kat Got Your Tongue · Missing Abby · Them* BS

## Beth Webb                                           Historical  Magic

Lian Hearn
Ursula Le Guin

Garth Nix
Michelle Paver

*Star Dancer*

## Catherine Webb                              Detective mysteries  Fantasy

Alison Croggon
Marianne Curley
Catherine Fisher
Diana Wynne Jones

Rhiannon Lassiter
Katherine Roberts
Eleanor Updale

*The Extraordinary & Unusual Adventures of Horatio Lyle*
*The Obsidian Dagger · Mirror Dreams · Mirror Wakes*
*Timekeepers · The Waywalkers*

💬 Some titles available as **Talking books**

12-14

## Robert Westall

Adventure  Ghost/supernatural
Science fiction  War 1939-45
8-11

Martin Booth
Michael Cronin
Peter Dickinson
Charlie Fletcher
Anthony Masters

Michael Morpurgo
Linda Newbery
James Riordan
Meg Rosoff
R L Stine

*Break of Dark · Gulf · The Promise*
*The Stones of Muncaster Cathedral · Urn Burial · The Watch House*

## Scott Westerfield

Science fiction  Social issues

Alison Allen-Grey
Ursula Le Guin

Garth Nix
Meg Rosoff

*Uglies · Pretties · Specials*
*Midnighters*

## Matt Whyman

Family  Other cultures  Social issues  Thrillers

Bernard Ashley
Kevin Brooks
Gillian Cross
Marianne Curley
Alan Gibbons

Jan Mark
Graham Marks
Mal Peet
Lee Weatherly

*Boy Kills Man · Superhuman · The Wild*

## Jacqueline Wilson 💬

Diaries  Family  Humour  Social issues

5-7 8-11

Raffaella Barker
Cathy Cassidy
Narinder Dhami
Anne Fine
Sandra Glover

Adeline Yen Mah
Helena Pielichaty
Bali Rai
Sue Townsend

*Girls in Love · Girls in Tears*
*Girls Out Late · Lola Rose · Love Lessons*

## Jeanette Winterson

Fantasy  Science fiction

Geraldine McCaughrean
Philip Pullman

Meg Rosoff

*Tanglewreck*

# Clive Woodall 💬
Animals  Fantasy

Brian Jacques

J R R Tolkien

*One for Sorrow • Seven for a Secret*

# Chris Wooding
Fantasy  Horror

Stephen Cole
Joseph Delaney
Ann Halam
Robin Jarvis
Garth Nix

Philip Reeve
Marcus Sedgwick
Darren Shan
Jonathan Stroud
Cate Tiernan

*The Haunting of Alaizabel Cray • Poison • The Storm Thief*

# Tim Wynne-Jones
Social issues  Thrillers

Alison Allen-Gray
Lynne Reid Banks

Suzanne Fisher Staples

*The Boy in the Burning House • The Survival Game*

# Rick Yancey
Mythology  Thrillers

Eoin Colfer
Joseph Delaney

Katherine Roberts

*The Extraordinary Adventures of Alfred Kropp*

# Benjamin Zephaniah
Other cultures  Social issues  War

Catherine Forde
Alan Gibbons
Gaye Hiçyilmaz

Joan Lingard
Beverley Naidoo
Robert Swindells

*Face • Gangsta Rap • Refugee Boy*

# Markus Zusak
Death  War 1939-45

John Boyne
Michael Cronin

Morris Gleitzman
Michael Morpurgo

*The Book Thief*

**12-14**

# Genres and Themes

## Adventure

Genres

### 5-7

Roy Apps
Phyllis Arkle
Martyn Beardsley
Malorie Blackman
Jon Blake
Benedict Blathwayt
Adrian Boote
Henrietta Branford
Herbie Brennan
Jeff Brown
Judy Brown
Lisa Bruce
Damon Burnard
Peter Clover
Andrew Cope

Jonathan Emmett
John Grant
Sally Grindley
Alex Gutteridge
Mary Hoffman
Mary Hooper
Julia Jarman
Ann Jungman
Peter Kavanagh
Diana Kimpton
Timothy Knapman
Elizabeth Lindsay
Sam McBratney
Marilyn McLaughlin
Colin McNaughton

Hilda Offen
Hiawyn Oram
Daniel Postgate
Chris Powling
Alf Prøysen
Shoo Rayner
Margaret Ryan
Dyan Sheldon
Dee Shulman
Emily Smith
Jeremy Strong
Ian Whybrow
David Henry Wilson
Jacqueline Wilson
Philip Wooderson

### 8-11

Deborah Abela
Joan Aiken
Roy Apps
Mary Arrigan
Paul Bajoria
Blue Balliett
Dominic Barker
Terence Blacker
Malorie Blackman
Enid Blyton
Lucy M Boston
Frank Cottrell Boyce
Tony Bradman
Henrietta Branford
Herbie Brennan
Linda Buckley-Archer
Georgia Byng
Simon Chapman
Michael Coleman
Eoin Colfer
Susan Cooper
W J Corbett
Zizou Corder
Helen Cresswell

Gillian Cross
Kevin Crossley-Holland
Chris d'Lacey
Anna Dale
Colin Dann
Berlie Doherty
Helen Dunmore
Alan Durant
John Fardell
Cornelia Funke
Alan Garner
Susan Gates
Carol Hedges
Hergé
Jason Hightman
Charlie Higson
Nigel Hinton
Michael Hoeye
Anthony Horowitz
Eva Ibbotson
Steve Jackson and
   Ian Livingstone
Brian Jacques
Allan Frewin Jones

P B Kerr
Garry Kilworth
Clive King
Elizabeth Laird
Penelope Lively
Sam Llewellyn
Mark McCorkle
Margaret Mahy
Jill Marshall
Anthony Masters
Michael Molloy
Michael Morpurgo
Joshua Mowll
William Nicholson
Mary Norton
Kenneth Oppel
Philippa Pearce
Stephen Potts
Chris Powling
Chris Priestley
Natalie Jane Prior
Philip Pullman
Arthur Ransome
Philip Reeve

# Adventure (cont)

## 8-11 (cont)

Justin Richards
Rick Riordan
Katherine Roberts
Emily Rodda
Sebastian Rook
Dyan Sheldon

Bowering Sivers
Dodie Smith
Robert Swindells
Alan Temperley
J R R Tolkien

Willy Vandersteen
Karen Wallace
Cat Weatherill
Robert Westall
Ursula Moray Williams

## 12-14

Joan Aiken
David Belbin
Martin Booth
A J Butcher
Susan Cooper
Joe Craig
Sharon Creech
Gillian Cross
Peter Dickinson
Paul Dowswell
Charlie Fletcher
Charlie Higson

Nigel Hinton
Mary Hoffman
Anthony Horowitz
Sam Hutton
Eva Ibbotson
Brian Jacques
Elizabeth Laird
Andy McNab and
    Robert Rigby
Catherine MacPhail
Anthony Masters

Michael Molloy
Joshua Mowll
Robert Muchamore
William Nicholson
Garth Nix
Meg Rosoff
Chris Ryan
Natsuki Takaya
G P Taylor
Karen Wallace
Robert Westall

# Animals

## 5-7

Anne Adeney
Allan Ahlberg
Giles Andreae
Phyllis Arkle
Henrietta Branford
Marc Brown
Nick Butterworth
Anne Cassidy
Harriet Castor
Emma Chichester Clark
Peter Clover
Andrew Cope
Chris d'Lacey
Jenny Dale
Lucy Daniels
Penny Dolan
Julia Donaldson
Joyce Dunbar

Vivian French
Neil Gaiman
Adèle Geras
Pippa Goodhart
Kes Gray
Sally Grindley
Kathy Henderson
Mary Hoffman
Rose Impey
Julia Jarman
Anita Jeram
Dick King-Smith
Tessa Krailing
Elizabeth Lindsay
Joan Lingard
Arnold Lobel
Geraldine McCaughrean
James Marshall

Anthony Masters
Nicola Moon
Michael Morpurgo
Jenny Nimmo
Hiawyn Oram
Beatrix Potter
Jillian Powell
Shoo Rayner
Hilary Robinson
Frank Rodgers
Alan Rusbridger
Angie Sage
Jill Tomlinson
Alison Uttley
Colin West
Ian Whybrow
Jeanne Willis
Selina Young

*Genres*

# Animals (cont)

## 8-11

Richard Adams
Antonia Barber
Michelle Bates
Julie Bertagna
Michael Bond
Betsy Byars
Kathryn Cave
Linda Chapman
David Clement-Davies
Louise Cooper
Andrew Cope
W J Corbett
Zizou Corder
Jenny Dale
Lucy Daniels
Colin Dann
Narinder Dhami

Kate di Camillo
Joshua Doder
Roddy Doyle
Kathleen Duey
Morris Gleitzman
Pippa Goodhart
Kenneth Grahame
Michael Hoeye
Mary Hooper
Brian Jacques
Deborah Kent
Garry Kilworth
Dick King-Smith
Elmore Leonard
Elizabeth Lindsay
Anthony Masters
Livi Michael

A A Milne
Linda Newbery
Jenny Oldfield
Kenneth Oppel
Michelle Paver
Philippa Pearce
Daniel Pennac
Angie Sage
S F Said
Anna Sewell
Alexander McCall
  Smith
Dodie Smith
Paul Stewart
Geronimo Stilton
E B White
Ursula Moray Williams

## 12-14

Michael Morpurgo

Kate Thompson

Clive Woodall

# Ballet

## 5-7

Antonia Barber
Ann Bryant
Harriet Castor
Adèle Geras
Anna Wilson

## 8-11

Antonia Barber
Adèle Geras
Alexandra Moss
Noel Streatfeild
Anna Wilson

## 12-14

Frances Mary Hendry

# Computers

## 8-11

Terence Blacker
Malorie Blackman
Michael Coleman

## 12-14

Terence Blacker
Malorie Blackman
Rhiannon Lassiter

# Crime

## 8-11
Frank Cottrell Boyce

## 12-14
Mark Haddon
Sam Hutton

Hervé Jubert
Eleanor Updale

# Death

## 5-7
Jeanne Willis

## 12-14
John Boyne
Brian Keaney
Anthony McGowan

Valerie Mendes
Nicola Morgan
Markus Zusak

Genres

# Detective mystery

## 5-7
Herbie Brennan

## 8-11
Deborah Abela
Cherith Baldry
Blue Balliett
Dominic Barker
Malorie Blackman
Thomas Bloor
Enid Blyton

Eoin Colfer
Allan Frewin Jones
Garry Kilworth
Caroline Lawrence
Barbara Mitchelhill
Chris Priestley

Anthony Read
Justin Richards
Emily Rodda
Alexander McCall
 Smith
Wendelin Van Draanen

## 12-14
Dominic Barker
Frank Cottrell Boyce
Meg Cabot

Anne Cassidy
Eoin Colfer
Sam Hutton

Hervé Jubert
Nicky Singer
Catherine Webb

# Diaries

## 5-7
Simon Bartram

## 8-11
Sharon Creech
Lucy Daniels
Anne Fine
Patricia Finney

Kelly McKain
Alexandra Moss
Helena Pielichaty
Richard Platt

Jamie Rix
Jean Ure
Ian Whybrow

137

# Diaries (cont)

## 12-14

Meg Cabot
Sharon Creech

Carolyn Meyer
Louise Rennison

Sue Townsend
Jacqueline Wilson

# Disability

## 12-14

Mark Haddon

Catherine MacPhail

James Riordan

Genres

# Environment

## 5-7

Kathy Henderson

## 8-11

Richard Adams
Tony Bradman
W J Corbett

Ted Hughes
Mia Ikumi

Clive King
Robert C O'Brien

## 12-14

Julie Bertagna
Matt Groening

Carl Hiaasen
Lesley Howarth

Marcus Sedgwick

# Fairy/folk

## 5-7

Anne Adeney
Tony Bradman
Anne Cassidy
Lauren Child
Malachy Doyle

Mini Grey
Karina Law
Maggie Moore
Michael Morpurgo

Margaret Nash
Barrie Wade
Karen Wallace
Chris Wormell

## 8-11

Ian Beck
Katherine Langrish
Geraldine McCaughrean

Gerald Morris
Eric Pringle

Philip Pullman
Gwyneth Rees

## 12-14

Adèle Geras

# Family

## 5-7

Allan Ahlberg
Jon Blake
Joyce Lankester Brisley
Marc Brown
Ann Cameron
Lauren Child
Chris d'Lacey
Helen Dunmore
Dorothy Edwards
Anne Fine
Neil Gaiman
Jamila Gavin
Adèle Geras
Kes Gray
Kathy Henderson
Mary Hooper

Shirley Hughes
Rose Impey
Dick King-Smith
Karina Law
Joan Lingard
Hilary McKay
Barbara Mitchelhill
Nicola Moon
Bel Mooney
Michael Morpurgo
Magdalen Nabb
Jenny Nimmo
Hilda Offen
Tony and Jan Payne
Daniel Postgate

Beatrix Potter
Jillian Powell
Chris Powling
Margaret Ryan
Angie Sage
Francesca Simon
Emily Smith
Wendy Smith
Paul Stewart
Jeremy Strong
Kaye Umansky
Karen Wallace
Colin West
David Henry Wilson
Jacqueline Wilson

## 8-11

Allan Ahlberg
Joan Aiken
Louisa May Alcott
David Almond
Rachel Anderson
Lynne Reid Banks
Nina Bawden
Ian Beck
Julie Bertagna
Jeanne Birdsall
Thomas Bloor
Judy Blume
Michael Bond
Lucy M Boston
Frank Cottrell Boyce
Christiana Brand
Frances Hodgson
  Burnett
Betsy Byars
Cathy Cassidy
Linda Chapman
Yvonne Coppard
Sharon Creech
Helen Cresswell
Richmal Crompton
Chris d'Lacey

Annie Dalton
Paula Danziger
Kate di Camillo
Berlie Doherty
Fiona Dunbar
Helen Dunmore
Anne Fine
Jack Gantos
Susan Gates
Jamila Gavin
Adèle Geras
Morris Gleitzman
Debi Gliori
Sally Grindley
Diana Hendry
Rose Impey
Julia Jarman
Tim Kennemore
Elizabeth Cody Kimmel
Dick King-Smith
Elizabeth Laird
Karen McCombie
Megan McDonald
Hilary McKay
Catherine MacPhail
Michelle Magorian

Margaret Mahy
Jan Mark
Simon Mason
Barbara Mitchelhill
L M Montgomery
Joshua Mowll
E Nesbit
Linda Newbery
Jenny Nimmo
Andrew Norriss
Mary Norton
Jenny Oldfield
Siobhán Parkinson
Philippa Pearce
Arthur Ransome
Philip Ridley
Margaret Ryan
Francesca Simon
Johanna Spyri
Noel Streatfeild
Jeremy Strong
Theresa Tomlinson
P L Travers
Laura Ingalls Wilder
Jacqueline Wilson

# Family (cont)

## 12-14

Alison Allen-Gray
David Almond
Rachel Anderson
Bernard Ashley
Ros Asquith
Raffaella Barker
Joan Bauer
Veronica Bennett
Malorie Blackman
Tim Bowler
Frank Cottrell Boyce
Theresa Breslin
Kevin Brooks
Melvin Burgess
Kate Cann
Cathy Cassidy
Gennifer Choldenko
Julia Clarke
Sharon Creech
Narinder Dhami
Berlie Doherty
Deborah Ellis

Josephine Feeney
Anne Fine
Adèle Geras
Alan Gibbons
Morris Gleitzman
Matt Groening
Mark Haddon
Carl Hiaasen
Gaye Hiçyilmaz
Nigel Hinton
Mary Hoffman
Mary Hooper
Cathy Hopkins
Lesley Howarth
Brian Keaney
Elizabeth Laird
Kathryn Lamb
Geraldine McCaughrean
Karen McCombie
Hilary McKay
Michelle Magorian

Adeline Yen Mah
Jan Mark
Graham Marks
Valerie Mendes
Joshua Mowll
Linda Newbery
Helena Pielichaty
Caroline Plaisted
Alison Prince
Chloë Rayban
Catherine Robinson
Meg Rosoff
Rosie Rushton
Alex Shearer
John Singleton
Jeff Smith
Marc Sumerak
Theresa Tomlinson
Jean Ure
Matt Whyman
Jacqueline Wilson

# Fantasy

## 5-7

Giles Andreae
Simon Bartram
Adrian Boote
Tony Bradman
Henrietta Branford
Jeff Brown
Judy Brown
Keith Brumpton
Linda Chapman
June Crebbin
Roald Dahl

Julia Donaldson
Anne Fine
Neil Gaiman
Sally Gardner
Pippa Goodhart
Mini Grey
Mary Hoffman
Oliver Jeffers
Ann Jungman
Dick King-Smith
Timothy Knapman

Megan McDonald
Kelly McKain
Jenny Nimmo
Alf Prøysen
Chris Riddell
Angie Sage
Jeremy Strong
Kaye Umansky
Jacqueline Wilson
Chris Wormell

## 8-11

Richard Adams
Allan Ahlberg
Joan Aiken

David Almond
Roy Apps
Steve Augarde

Lynne Reid Banks
Dominic Barker
J M Barrie

# Fantasy (cont)

## 8-11 (cont)

Frank L Baum
Luc Besson
Holly Black
Lucy M Boston
Stephen Bowkett
Theresa Breslin
Raymond Briggs
Melvin Burgess
Georgia Byng
Lewis Carroll
Kathryn Cave
Linda Chapman
David Clement-Davies
Eoin Colfer
Louise Cooper
Susan Cooper
Zizou Corder
Bruce Coville
Cressida Cowell
Helen Cresswell
Chris d'Lacey
Roald Dahl
Annie Dalton
Berlie Doherty
Malachy Doyle
Kathleen Duey
Jeanne DuPrau
Stephen Elboz
Catherine Fisher
Charlie Fletcher
Cornelia Funke
Neil Gaiman
Alan Garner
Susan Gates
Jamila Gavin
Alan Gibbons

Debi Gliori
Julia Golding
John Gordon
Simon Goswell
Elizabeth Goudge
Kenneth Grahame
Kes Gray
Diana Hendry
Jason Hightman
Nigel Hinton
Michael Hoeye
Lesley Howarth
Ted Hughes
Eva Ibbotson
Mia Ikumi
Steve Jackson and
  Ian Livingstone
Brian Jacques
Robin Jarvis
Paul Jennings
Diana Wynne Jones
Elizabeth Kay
P B Kerr
Garry Kilworth
Katherine Langrish
Michael Lawrence
Elmore Leonard
C S Lewis
Penelope Lively
Geraldine McCaughrean
Hazel Marshall
Livi Michael
Michael Molloy
Joshua Mowll
Jill Murphy
E Nesbit

William Nicholson
Jenny Nimmo
Andrew Norriss
Mary Norton
Robert C O'Brien
Ian Ogilvy
Kenneth Oppel
Michelle Paver
Philippa Pearce
Stephen Potts
Terry Pratchett
Susan Price
Philip Pullman
Celia Rees
Philip Ridley
Katherine Roberts
Emily Rodda
J K Rowling
Kate Saunders
Matthew Skelton
Lemony Snicket
Justin Somper
Paul Stewart
David Lee Stone
Alan Temperley
Kate Thompson
J R R Tolkien
Theresa Tomlinson
P L Travers
Val Tyler
Steve Voake
John Vornholt
Cat Weatherill
E B White
T H White
Ursula Moray Williams

## 12-14

Joan Aiken
Lloyd Alexander
David Almond
Dominic Barker
Julie Bertagna

Holly Black
Stephen Bowkett
Theresa Breslin
N M Browne
Trudi Canavan

Ann Coburn
Eoin Colfer
Louise Cooper
Susan Cooper
Alison Croggon

*Genres*

# Fantasy (cont)

## 12-14 (cont)

Marianne Curley
John Dickinson
Peter Dickinson
Stephen Elboz
Catherine Fisher
Charlie Fletcher
Susan Gates
Carlo Gebler
Alan Gibbons
Shannon Hale
Victoria Hanley
Frances Hardinge
Lian Hearn
Stuart Hill
Nigel Hinton
Mary Hoffman
Brian Jacques
Robin Jarvis
Pete Johnson
Diana Wynne Jones

Hervé Jubert
Hope Larson
Rhiannon Lassiter
Michael Lawrence
Ursula Le Guin
Tanith Lee
Geraldine McCaughrean
Cliff McNish
Catherine MacPhail
Margaret Mahy
Jan Mark
Andrew Matthews
Kai Meyer
Nicola Morgan
Joshua Mowll
Ted Naifeh
William Nicholson
Garth Nix
Christopher Paolini
Michelle Paver

Tamora Pierce
Terry Pratchett
Susan Price
Sally Prue
Philip Pullman
Philip Reeve
Katherine Roberts
J K Rowling
Mathew Skelton
Dugald Steer
David Lee Stone
Jonathan Stroud
G P Taylor
Kate Thompson
J R R Tolkien
Catherine Webb
Jeanette Winterson
Clive Woodall
Chris Wooding

# Friends

## 5-7

Giles Andreae
Antonia Barber
Marc Brown
Lisa Bruce
Ann Bryant
Ann Cameron
Harriet Castor
Emma Chichester Clark
Michael Coleman
John Cunliffe

Lucy Daniels
Joyce Dunbar
Helen Dunmore
Dorothy Edwards
Jonathan Emmett
Anne Fine
Jamila Gavin
Sally Grindley
Oliver Jeffers
Tessa Krailing

Hilary McKay
Marilyn McLaughlin
Magdalen Nabb
Jenny Oldfield
Dyan Sheldon
Emily Smith
Wendy Smith
Anna Wilson
Bob Wilson
Selina Young

## 8-11

Louise Arnold
Ros Asquith
David Bedford
Ann Bryant
Helen Dunmore
Charlie Fletcher

Sandra Glover
Meg Harper
Mia Ikumi
Karen McCombie
Kelly McKain
Daisy Meadows
Siobhán Parkinson

Helena Pielichaty
Caroline Plaisted
Bali Rai
Jennie Walters
Holly Webb
Cherry Whytock
Anna Wilson

# Friends (cont)

## 12-14

Sherry Ashworth
Raffaella Barker
Joan Bauer
Ann Brashares
Meg Cabot
Kate Cann
Charlie Fletcher
Catherine Forde

Jamila Gavin
Sandra Glover
Keith Gray
Mary Hooper
Kathryn Lamb
Sue Limb
Karen McCombie
Andrew Matthews

Sue Mayfield
Robert Muchamore
James Patterson
James Riordan
Catherine Robinson
Natsuki Takaya
Karen Wallace
Lee Weatherly

# Ghost/supernatural

## 5-7

Scoular Anderson
Tony Bradman
June Crebbin

Penny Dolan
Anne Fine
Anthony Masters

Barbara Mitchelhill
Chris Powling
Dee Shulman

## 8-11

Joan Aiken
Louise Arnold
Mary Arrigan
Melvin Burgess
Sharon Creech
Bridget Crowley
Joseph Delaney
Griselda Gifford
Pippa Goodhart

John Gordon
Mary Hooper
Eva Ibbotson
Julia Jarman
Pete Johnson
Diana Wynne Jones
Penelope Lively
Margaret Mahy

Anthony Masters
Jenny Nimmo
Susan Price
Celia Rees
Robert Swindells
Kate Thompson
Jean Ure
Robert Westall

## 12-14

Joan Aiken
David Almond
Joseph Delaney
Peter Dickinson
Sandra Glover
Ann Halam

Julie Hearn
Eva Ibbotson
Paul Jennings
Pete Johnson
Cliff McNish
Anthony Masters

Andrew Matthews
Susan Price
Celia Rees
Marcus Sedgwick
Nicky Singer
Robert Westall

# Historical

C17th 17th Century  ·  M Medieval  ·  R Roman
T Tudor  ·  V Victorian  ·  Vk Viking

## 5-7

Scoular Anderson
Keith Brumpton
Malachy Doyle

John Grant
Dennis Hamley
Mary Hooper

Anthony Masters
Philip Wooderson

## 8-11

Roy Apps
Mary Arrigan
Paul Bajoria
Cherith Baldry M
Theresa Breslin
Linda Buckley-Archer
Frances Hodgson
  Burnett V
Susan Cooper
Cressida Cowell
Kevin Crossley-Holland M
Terry Deary
Berlie Doherty

Paul Dowswell V
Patricia Finney T
Sally Gardner
René Goscinny R
Hergé
Mary Hooper
Julia Jarman
Deborah Kent
Katherine Langrish Vk
Caroline Lawrence R
Geraldine McCaughrean
Hazel Marshall
Michael Molloy V

Michael Morpurgo
Gerald Morris M
Richard Platt
Chris Priestley
Anthony Read V
Justin Richards
Paul Shipton
Bowering Sivers V
Dugald Steer
Rosemary Sutcliff M R
Theresa Tomlinson
Karen Wallace

## 12-14

Joan Aiken
Martin Booth
N M Browne R
Pauline Chandler
Kevin Crossley-Holland M
Berlie Doherty
Jennifer Donnelly
Paul Dowswell V
Nancy Farmer
Aubrey Flegg
Sally Gardner C17th
Susan Gates
Jamila Gavin
Carlo Gebler
Adèle Geras

Julie Hearn
Lian Hearn
Frances Mary Hendry R
Mary Hoffman
Mary Hooper
Ben Jeapes
Geraldine McCaughrean
Jan Mark T
Graham Marks V
Carolyn Meyer T
Michael Molloy V
Nicola Morgan
Michael Morpurgo
Donna Jo Napoli
Joan O'Neill

Kate Pennington T V
K M Peyton
Alison Prince V
Maggie Prince
Philip Pullman V
Celia Rees
Marcus Sedgwick
Mildred D Taylor
Theresa Tomlinson
Ann Turnbull
Eleanor Updale
Karen Wallace
Jennie Walters V
Beth Webb

Genres

# Horror

## 8-11

Sam Llewellyn
Sebastian Rook

Nick Shadow
Justin Somper

R L Stine
Alan Temperley

## 12-14

Stephen Cole
Catherine Fisher
Nick Gifford
Ann Halam
Anthony Horowitz

Erik L'Homme
Anthony Masters
E E Richardson
Nick Shadow

Darren Shan
R L Stine
G P Taylor
Chris Wooding

# Humour

## 5-7

Anne Adeney
Allan Ahlberg
Jonathan Allen
Scoular Anderson
Giles Andreae
Laurence Anholt
Roy Apps
Martyn Beardsley
Stan and Jan
  Berenstain
Terence Blacker
Andy Blackford
Jon Blake
Adrian Boote
Tony Bradman
Herbie Brennan
Raymond Briggs
Joyce Lankester Brisley
Marc Brown
Keith Brumpton
Janet Burchett and
  Sara Vogler
Damon Burnard
Nick Butterworth
Ann Cameron
Humphrey Carpenter
Anne Cassidy
Lauren Child
Emma Chichester Clark

Michael Coleman
Andrew Cope
June Crebbin
John Cunliffe
Chris d'Lacey
Roald Dahl
Penny Dolan
Malachy Doyle
Joyce Dunbar
Alan Durant
P D Eastman
Dorothy Edwards
Jonathan Emmett
Jan Fearnley
Vivian French
Sue Graves
Emily Gravett
Kes Gray
Mini Grey
Alex Gutteridge
Dave Hanson
Damian Harvey
Mary Hoffman
Mary Hooper
Shirley Hughes
Rose Impey
Julia Jarman
Oliver Jeffers
Anita Jeram

Ann Jungman
Dick King-Smith
Karina Law
Theo Le Sieg
Arnold Lobel
Sam McBratney
Geraldine McCaughrean
Megan McDonald
Marilyn McLaughlin
Colin McNaughton
James Marshall
Anthony Masters
Barbara Mitchelhill
Tony Mitton
Nicola Moon
Bel Mooney
Maggie Moore
Jill Murphy
Margaret Nash
Jenny Oldfield
Hiawyn Oram
Tony and Jan Payne
Dav Pilkey
Daniel Postgate
Jillian Powell
Chris Powling
Alf Prøysen
Shoo Rayner
Chris Riddell

# Humour (cont)

## 5-7 (cont)

Hilary Robinson
Frank Rodgers
Alan Rusbridger
Margaret Ryan
Louis Sachar
Angie Sage
Dr Seuss
Nick Sharratt
Dyan Sheldon

Dee Shulman
Francesca Simon
Emily Smith
Wendy Smith
Paul Stewart
Jeremy Strong
Jill Tomlinson
Kaye Umansky
Barrie Wade

Karen Wallace
Colin West
Ian Whybrow
Jeanne Willis
Bob Wilson
David Henry Wilson
Jacqueline Wilson
Philip Wooderson
Selina Young

## 8-11

Allan Ahlberg
Giles Andreae
Laurence Anholt
Roy Apps
Philip Ardagh
Ros Asquith
Dominic Barker
Steve Barlow and
   Steve Skidmore
Martyn Beardsley
Julie Bertagna
Terence Blacker
Judy Blume
Frank Cottrell Boyce
Christiana Brand
Henrietta Branford
Herbie Brennan
Theresa Breslin
Raymond Briggs
Ann Bryant
Betsy Byars
Georgia Byng
Kathryn Cave
Lauren Child
Steve Cole
Eoin Colfer
Andrew Cope
Yvonne Coppard
Bruce Coville
Cressida Cowell
Sharon Creech
Helen Cresswell

Richmal Crompton
Gillian Cross
Roald Dahl
Paula Danziger
Terry Deary
Joshua Doder
Roddy Doyle
Alan Durant
Heather Dyer
Anne Fine
Neil Gaiman
Susan Gates
Morris Gleitzman
Debi Gliori
René Goscinny
Kes Gray
Andy Griffiths
Mark Haddon
Meg Harper
Michael Hoeye
Mary Hooper
Anthony Horowitz
Eva Ibbotson
Rose Impey
Paul Jennings
Pete Johnson
Gene Kemp
Elizabeth Cody Kimmel
Dick King-Smith
Michael Lawrence
Sam Llewellyn
Karen McCombie

Megan McDonald
Kelly McKain
Hilary McKay
Catherine MacPhail
Margaret Mahy
Jan Mark
Simon Mason
Livi Michael
Barbara Mitchelhill
Jill Murphy
Andrew Norriss
Ian Ogilvy
Jenny Oldfield
Siobhán Parkinson
Dav Pilkey
Terry Pratchett
Eric Pringle
Natalie Jane Prior
Shoo Rayner
Philip Reeve
Philip Ridley
Rick Riordan
Jamie Rix
David Roberts
Margaret Ryan
Louis Sachar
Dyan Sheldon
Paul Shipton
Francesca Simon
Alexander McCall Smith
Lemony Snicket
Geronimo Stilton

# Humour (cont)

## 8-11 (cont)

Jeremy Strong
P L Travers
Kaye Umansky

Wendelin Van Draanen
Ian Whybrow
David Henry Wilson

Jacqueline Wilson
Ceri Worman

## 12-14

Ros Asquith
Dominic Barker
Frank Cottrell Boyce
Meg Cabot
Anne Fine
Morris Gleitzman
Matt Groening
Carl Hiaasen
Cathy Hopkins
Anthony Horowitz

Eva Ibbotson
Paul Jennings
Susan Juby
Kathryn Lamb
Sue Limb
Karen McCombie
Anthony McGowan
Hilary McKay
Caroline Plaisted
Terry Pratchett

Sally Prue
Louise Rennison
Rosie Rushton
Louis Sachar
Jeff Smith
David Lee Stone
Jeremy Strong
Sue Townsend
Jacqueline Wilson

# Illness

## 8-11

Rachel Anderson

## 12-14

Rachel Anderson
Anthony McGowan

Linda Newbery
John Singleton

# Letters

## 5-7

Ian Whybrow

## 8-11

Herbie Brennan
Sally Grindley

Harry Horse
Helena Pielichaty

Jean Ure
Ian Whybrow

## 12-14

Rosie Rushton

# Magic

### 5-7

Jonathan Allen
Scoular Anderson
Roy Apps
Terence Blacker
Malorie Blackman
Humphrey Carpenter
Linda Chapman
Jonathan Emmett
Maeve Friel

Alex Gutteridge
Julia Jarman
Ann Jungman
Peter Kavanagh
Elizabeth Lindsay
Kelly McKain
Daisy Meadows
Jill Murphy
Jenny Nimmo

Jenny Oldfield
Hiawyn Oram
Ghillian Potts
Alf Prøysen
Gwyneth Rees
Frank Rodgers
Margaret Ryan
Wendy Smith
Kaye Umansky

### 8-11

E D Baker
Linda Chapman
Louise Cooper
Cressida Cowell
Anna Dale
Joseph Delaney
Fiona Dunbar
Heather Dyer
Stephen Elboz

Maeve Friel
Sally Gardner
Debi Gliori
Diana Wynne Jones
Elizabeth Kay
Tim Kennemore
Elizabeth Lindsay
Daisy Meadows
Jill Murphy

Alf Prøysen
Gwyneth Rees
J K Rowling
Angie Sage
Dugald Steer
Alan Temperley
P L Travers
Kaye Umansky
Cat Weatherill

### 12-14

Trudi Canavan
Ann Coburn
Marianne Curley
Joseph Delaney
Stephen Elboz
Sally Gardner
Erik L'Homme

Hope Larson
Ursula Le Guin
Cliff McNish
Ted Naifeh
Tamora Pierce
Maggie Prince

J K Rowling
Mathew Skelton
Dugald Steer
G P Taylor
Cate Tiernan
Beth Webb

# Mystery

### 12-14

Alison Allen-Gray
Kevin Brooks
Mal Peet

Kate Pennington
Tom Pow

M E Rabb
Marcus Sedgwick

# Mythology

## 5-7

Jamila Gavin
Geraldine McCaughrean

Margaret Mayo
Tony Mitton

Saviour Pirotta
Karen Wallace

## 8-11

Steve Barlow and
  Steve Skidmore
Kevin Crossley-Holland
Terry Deary

Ted Hughes
Rick Riordan
Katherine Roberts

Paul Shipton
Rosemary Sutcliff
T H White

## 12-14

N M Browne
Melvin Burgess
Kevin Crossley-Holland

Nancy Farmer
Carlo Gebler
Susan Price

Katherine Roberts
Dugald Steer
Rick Yancey

# Other cultures

## 5-7

Lisa Bruce

Ann Cameron

Jamila Gavin

## 8-11

Bob Cattell
Sally Grindley
Elizabeth Laird

Joshua Mowll
Bali Rai

Alexander McCall Smith
Sandi Toksvig

## 12-14

Lynne Reid Banks
Deborah Ellis
Nancy Farmer
Aubrey Flegg
Susan Gates
Jamila Gavin
Philip Gross
Lian Hearn

Gaye Hiçyilmaz
Elizabeth Laird
Geraldine McCaughrean
Adeline Yen Mah
Henning Mankell
Kai Meyer
Joshua Mowll

Donna Jo Napoli
Bali Rai
Dyan Sheldon
Suzanne Fisher Staples
Jean Ure
Matt Whyman
Benjamin Zephaniah

# Other lands

### 5-7
Malorie Blackman

### 8-11
Kate di Camillo

Geraldine McCaughrean

Laura Ingalls Wilder

Jamila Gavin

### 12-14
Lynne Reid Banks

Beverley Naidoo

Mildred D Taylor

Deborah Ellis

Suzanne Fisher Staples

Genres

# Pony/horse

### 5-7
Linda Chapman
Peter Clover
Diana Kimpton
Elizabeth Lindsay

### 8-11
Jenny Oldfield
Anna Sewell

### 12-14
Hope Larson
K M Peyton

# Romance

### 12-14
Ros Asquith

Susan Juby

Dyan Sheldon

Veronica Bennett

Chloë Rayban

Jerry Spinelli

Jennifer Donnelly

Louise Rennison

Ann Turnbull

Cathy Hopkins

Catherine Robinson

Jean Ure

Pete Johnson

# School

### 5-7
Terence Blacker

Sam McBratney

Dyan Sheldon

Humphrey Carpenter

Jenny Oldfield

Francesca Simon

Rob Childs

Ghillian Potts

Anna Wilson

Michael Coleman

Jillian Powell

Bob Wilson

# School (cont)

## 8-11

Blue Balliett
Judy Blume
Enid Blyton
Elinor M Brent-Dyer
Ann Bryant
Lauren Child
Richmal Crompton
Gillian Cross

Narinder Dhami
Helen Dunmore
Anne Fine
Jackie French
Jack Gantos
Cindy Jefferies
Gene Kemp
Kelly McKain

Alexandra Moss
Jill Murphy
Helena Pielichaty
Bali Rai
J K Rowling
Louis Sachar
Jean Ure
Anna Wilson

## 12-14

Ros Asquith
Raffaella Barker
Veronica Bennett
Gillian Cross
Josephine Feeney

Anne Fine
Graham Gardner
Adèle Geras
Bali Rai
J K Rowling

Louis Sachar
Dyan Sheldon
Jerry Spinelli
Marc Sumerak

# Science fiction

## 5-7

Malorie Blackman

Sam McBratney

Paul Stewart

## 8-11

Rachel Anderson
Neil Arksey
Steve Cole
Bruce Coville

Bridget Crowley
Jeanne DuPrau
Lesley Howarth
Jenny Nimmo

Andrew Norriss
Justin Richards
S F Said
Robert Swindells

## 12-14

Alison Allen-Gray
Terence Blacker
Melvin Burgess
Stephen Cole
Louise Cooper
Susan Gates
Matt Groening

Ben Jeapes
Rhiannon Lassiter
James Patterson
Tom Pow
Susan Price
Alex Shearer

Marc Sumerak
Robert Swindells
Kate Thompson
Robert Westall
Scott Westerfield
Jeanette Winterson

# Sea/boats

## 8-11

Susan Cooper
Paul Dowswell
Michael Molloy
Stephen Potts

## 12-14

Paul Dowswell

# Social issues

## 8-11

Julie Bertagna
Malorie Blackman
Melvin Burgess
Georgia Byng
Cathy Cassidy
Chris d'Lacey
Jack Gantos
Alan Gibbons

Griselda Gifford
Diana Hendry
Lesley Howarth
Elizabeth Laird
Hilary McKay
Catherine MacPhail
Jan Mark
Michael Morpurgo

Linda Newbery
Kenneth Oppel
Stephen Potts
Celia Rees
Louis Sachar
Theresa Tomlinson
Jacqueline Wilson

## 12-14

David Almond
Rachel Anderson
Bernard Ashley
Sherry Ashworth
Lynne Reid Banks
Joan Bauer
David Belbin
Veronica Bennett
Julie Bertagna
Terence Blacker
Malorie Blackman
Tim Bowler
John Boyne
Theresa Breslin
Kevin Brooks
Melvin Burgess
Kate Cann
Anne Cassidy
Cathy Cassidy
Patrick Cave
Gennifer Choldenko
Julia Clarke
Gillian Cross
Narinder Dhami
Peter Dickinson
Berlie Doherty
Anne Fine
Aubrey Flegg
Catherine Forde
Graham Gardner
Alan Gibbons

Morris Gleitzman
Sandra Glover
Keith Gray
Julia Green
Mark Haddon
Sonya Hartnett
Julie Hearn
Carl Hiaasen
Gaye Hiçyilmaz
S E Hinton
Mary Hooper
Cathy Hopkins
Pete Johnson
Susan Juby
Brian Keaney
Elizabeth Laird
Kathryn Lamb
Joan Lingard
Karen McCombie
Anthony McGowan
Hilary McKay
Catherine MacPhail
Margaret Mahy
Henning Mankell
Jan Mark
Graham Marks
Sue Mayfield
Nicola Morgan
Beverley Naidoo
Linda Newbery
Joan O'Neill

James Patterson
Mal Peet
K M Peyton
Helena Pielichaty
Sally Prue
Philip Pullman
Celia Rees
James Riordan
Catherine Robinson
Malcolm Rose
Meg Rosoff
Rosie Rushton
Chris Ryan
Louis Sachar
Alex Shearer
Dyan Sheldon
Nicky Singer
John Singleton
Jerry Spinelli
Jeremy Strong
Jonathan Stroud
Robert Swindells
Kate Thompson
Jean Ure
Karen Wallace
Lee Weatherly
Scott Westerfield
Matt Whyman
Jacqueline Wilson
Tim Wynne-Jones
Benjamin Zephaniah

Genres

# Space

## 8-11
Mark Haddon

# Sport

## 5-7
Janet Burchett and
Sara Vogler

Rob Childs
Michael Coleman

Martin Waddell
Bob Wilson

## 8-11
Neil Arksey
David Bedford
Terence Blacker
Tony Bradman

Bob Cattell
Rob Childs
Michael Coleman

Narinder Dhami
Alan Durant
Alan Gibbons

## 12-14
Narinder Dhami

Mal Peet

# Stage

## 8-11
Antonia Barber

Julia Golding

Noel Streatfeild

# Thrillers

## 8-11
Paul Bajoria
Cathy Cassidy
Gillian Cross

Catherine Fisher
Sandra Glover
Pete Johnson

Chris Priestley
Sebastian Rook

## 12-14
Bernard Ashley
Sherry Ashworth
David Belbin
Malorie Blackman
Martin Booth
A J Butcher
Anne Cassidy
Cathy Cassidy
Patrick Cave
Stephen Cole
Eoin Colfer
Joe Craig
Gillian Cross

Catherine Fisher
Catherine Forde
Nick Gifford
Philip Gross
Nigel Hinton
Anthony Horowitz
Lesley Howarth
Sam Hutton
Ben Jeapes
Paul Jennings
Hervé Jubert
Penny Kendal
Andy McNab and
Robert Rigby

Graham Marks
Anthony Masters
Robert Muchamore
Philip Pullman
M E Rabb
Celia Rees
Malcolm Rose
Chris Ryan
Robert Swindells
Matt Whyman
Tim Wynne-Jones
Rick Yancey

# Traditional

## 5-7
Rose Impey

## 8-11
Kevin Crossley-Holland

# Transport

## 5-7
Benedict Blathwayt

# War
### WWI 1914-18 · WWII 1939-45

## 5-7
Helen Dunmore WWII          Dennis Hamley WWII

## 8-11

Rachel Anderson WWII    Morris Gleitzman WWII    Michael Morpurgo WWII
Steve Augarde          Sally Grindley WWII      Linda Newbery WWII
Nina Bawden WWII        Dennis Hamley WWII       Ian Serraillier WWII
Terry Deary WWII        Anne Holm WWII           Robert Swindells WWII
Paul Dowswell          Judith Kerr WWII         Sandi Toksvig WWII
Jackie French WWII      Michelle Magorian WWII   Robert Westall WWII
Griselda Gifford WWII

## 12-14

Rachel Anderson        Carlo Gebler WWII        Linda Newbery WWI
Bernard Ashley         Morris Gleitzman WWII    Joan O'Neill WWII
Martin Booth WWII      Shannon Hale             Alison Prince WWII
John Boyne WWII        Joan Lingard             Meg Rosoff
Theresa Breslin WWI    Michelle Magorian WWII   Jerry Spinelli WWII
Michael Cronin WWII    Adeline Yen Mah WWII     Robert Swindells
Deborah Ellis          Andrew Matthews WWI      Robert Westall WWII
Aubrey Flegg WWII      Michael Morpurgo WWII    Benjamin Zephaniah
                       Donna Jo Napoli WWII     Markus Zusak WWII

# The Rise of the Graphic Novel

The last five years have seen the integration of graphic novels into the mainstream. Librarians and booksellers have worked hard to try and meet the demand for this format. Some publishers are also reproducing already successful titles in a graphic novel format in an attempt to meet a wider audience and we have included some of these in the general age group guide.

The work done by a number of pioneering librarians around the country has shown the benefits of the graphic novel, particularly in terms of attracting teenage boys to books and reading. This has been further developed by a successful marketing campaign undertaken by the Reading Agency with one of the leading graphic novel publishers, Manga, to promote the young adult series Tokyopop. Many of their leading titles have female characters which has had the benefit of developing a strong female fan base.

The use of pictures seems to make any violence more real and the general style that some illustrators use, seeming to make the women characters more sexual, means that many of the books are in the older age range of the teen market. We have tried to pick a few of the series and titles suitable for the age groups targeted in 'Who Next' and which are available either through specialist outlets or some libraries. Please be aware that the quality and suitability of an individual book may vary because many series have a number of different authors and illustrators; where this happens below no authors are listed.

| Series/title | Author | Publisher |
| --- | --- | --- |
| Asterix | Rene Goscinny | Orion |
| Bone | Jeff Smith | HarperCollins |
| Chronicles of Conan | Roy Thomas | Titan Books |
| Courtney Cumrin | Ted Naifeh | Oni Press |
| Essential Avengers | | Marvel Comics Ltd |
| Essential X-Men | Chris Claremont | Marvel Comics Ltd |

| Series/title | Author | Publisher |
|---|---|---|
| *Exiles Series* | Tony Bedard | Marvel Comics Ltd |
| *Fruits Basket* | Natsuki Takaya | Tokyopop, Manga |
| *Futurama* | Matt Groening | HarperCollins |
| *.Hack/Legend of the Twilight* | Rei Izumi Tatsuya Hamazaki | Tokyopop, Manga |
| *The Greatest Adventures of Spike and Suzy* | Willy Vandersteen | Intes International |
| *Hellboy* | | Titan books |
| *Louis* | Metaphrog | Metaphrog |
| *The Simpsons* | Matt Groening | Titan Books |
| *Spider-Man* | | Marvel Publishing |
| *Star Trek* | | Titan Books |
| *Star Wars*    *Clone Wars Adventures*    *Dark Empire*    *Infinities* | | Titan Books |
| *ThunderCats* | | DC Comics |
| *Tintin* | Hergé | Egmont |
| *Tokyo Mew Mew* | Mia Ikumi | Tokyopop, Manga |
| *Ultimate Fantastic Four* | Mark Miller Ellis Warren | Marvel Publishing |
| *The Uncanny X-Men* | Chris Claremont | Marvel Comics Ltd |
| *Wallace and Gromit* | Dan Abnett Nick Newman Ian Rimmer | Titan Books |
| *X-Files* | Kevin Anderson | Checker |
| *X-Men Powerpack* | Marc Sumerak | Marvel Publishing |

# Current Children's Book Prizes

Since the last edition of this book the number of awards for children's books has proliferated. Many local Schools Library Services and public library authorities now run ballots locally, involving young people within their areas in voting for their favourite children's books in various categories. Examples of authorities presenting local awards include Berkshire, Doncaster, Lancashire, Medway, Nottingham, Portsmouth, Stockport, Stockton, Rotherham and Sussex. Some of the winners of these awards are listed on the Booktrust website whilst others may be accessed by looking at the authority's website. Some of the awards have their own website.

## Hans Christian Andersen Awards — Biennial

The highest international recognition given to authors and illustrators, these awards are presented to those whose complete works have made a lasting contribution to children's literature. The nominations are made by the national sections of IBBY, an international jury of children's literature specialists selects winners and the awards are presented during the biennial IBBY Congress. For further information contact: International Board on Books for Young People, Nonmenwag 12, Postfach CH-4003-Basel, Switzerland, tel: (+4161) 272 2917, email: ibby@eye.ch.

| | Author | Illustrator |
|---|---|---|
| 2006 | Margaret Mahy, New Zealand | Wolf Erlbruch, Germany |
| 2004 | Martin Waddell, Ireland | Max Velthuijs, The Netherlands |

## Angus Book Award — Annual

An Angus-wide initiative to encourage pupils aged 13/15 to read and enjoy quality teenage fiction. From January to May, third year pupils read the five titles shortlisted by teachers and librarians from books written by UK resident authors and published in paperback in the preceding 12 months. The children discuss the books before they vote in a secret ballot. For further details contact: Moyra Hood, Educational Resources Librarian, Bruce House, Wellgate, Arbroath DD11 3TL tel: 01241 435045, email:hoodm@angus.gov.uk.

2006 *TWOC* by Graham Joyce (Faber)

2005 *Boy 2 Girl* by Terence Blacker (Macmillan)

2004 *The Edge* by Alan Gibbons (Orion)

2003 *Warehouse* by Keith Gray (Red Fox)

## Askews Torchlight Children's Book Award Annual

This award aims to highlight quality fiction for 9 to 12 year olds, written by authors who have not already been shortlisted for major awards. The shortlist is selected by children's literature professionals and then children from Years 5, 6 and 7 are invited to vote for their favourite book from the shortlist, either by post or email: mail@askews.co.uk. For further details contact: Rob Sanderson, Askews Children's Book Award, Askews Library Services Ltd, 218-222 North Road, Preston, Lancashire PR1 1SY, tel: 01772 490 489, email: roberts@askews.co.uk.

2006　*The Lightning Thief* by Rick Riordan (Puffin)

2005　*Inkheart* by Cornelia Funke (Chicken House)

2004　*How to Train Your Dragon* by Cressida Cowell (Hodder)

2003　*The Thief Lord* by Cornelia Funke (Chicken House)

## Blue Peter Children's Book Awards Annual

Launched in 2000, the Blue Peter Book Awards are run by the BBC children's programme Blue Peter. A celebrity judging panel selects the shortlists from paperback titles published in the UK in the previous year. These books are then read by Blue Peter Young Judges chosen as a result of a Blue Peter Book Review Competition. They chose the winners for each of three categories. From these three winning titles, a Book of the Year is selected. For further information contact: Fraser Ross Associates, 6 Wellington Street, Edinburgh EH6 7EQ, tel: 0131 5532759 or fax: 0131 6574412.

2006　The Book I Couldn't Put Down
　　　*Blood Fever* by Charles Higson (Puffin)

　　　The Best Illustrated Book to Read Aloud and the
　　　**Blue Peter Book of the Year Award 2006**
　　　*Lost and Found* by Oliver Jeffers (HarperCollins)

　　　The Best Book with Facts
　　　*Spud Goes Green* by Giles Thaxton (Egmont)

2005　The Book I couldn't put down and the
　　　**Blue Peter Book of the Year Award 2005**
　　　*Private Peaceful* by Michael Morpurgo (Collins)

　　　The Best Illustrated Book to Read Aloud
　　　*The Snail and the Whale* by Julia Donaldson (Macmillan)

　　　The Best Book with Facts
　　　*Explorers Wanted! At the North Pole* by Simon Chapman (Egmont)

## Blue Peter Children's Book Awards (cont) Annual

2004 The Book I Couldn't Put Down
*Montmorency* by Eleanor Updale (Scholastic)

The Best Illustrated Book to Read Aloud and the
**Blue Peter Book of the Year Award 2004**
*Man on the Moon* by Simon Bartram (Templar)

The Best Book with Facts
*The Ultimate Book Guide* by Daniel Hahn & Leonie Flynn editors
(*A & C Black*)

2003 The Book I Couldn't Put Down and the
**Blue Peter Book of the Year Award 2003**
*Mortal Engines* by Philip Reeve (Scholastic)

The Best Illustrated Book to Read Aloud
*Room on the Broom* by Julia Donaldson & Axel Scheffler
(Macmillan)

The Best Book with Facts
*Pirate Diary* by Richard Platt & Chris Riddell (Walker)

## Branford Boase Award Annual

This award began in 2000 and is in memory of two very important figures
in the children's book world, both of whom died of cancer in 1999.
Henrietta Branford was a talented, award-winning children's novelist
and Wendy Boase was a passionate children's book editor who was the
Editorial Director of Walker Books as well as being one of its founders.
Supported by several publishers, headed by Walker Books, this annual
prize is awarded to an outstanding first-time novel for children. For
further details contact the administrator Anne Marley,
tel: 01962 826658, email: anne.marley@tiscali.co.uk.

2006 *Fly by Night* by Frances Hardinge (Macmillan)
2005 *How I Live Now* by Meg Rosoff (Puffin)
2004 *Keeper* by Mal Peet (Walker)
2003 *Martyn Pig* by Kevin Brooks (Chicken House)
2002 *Cold Tom* Sue Prue (Oxford University Press)

Prizes

# Carnegie and Greenaway Awards

The Carnegie and Kate Greenaway awards are presented annually by CILIP (Chartered Institute of Library and Information Professionals) and administered by the Youth Libraries Group of CILIP. Nominations are submitted by institute members and winners selected by a panel of 13 children's librarians from the Youth Libraries Group.

## Carnegie Medal
Annual

Instituted in 1936, the Carnegie Medal is given for an outstanding book for children. Contenders are appraised for characterisation, plot, style, accuracy, imaginative quality and that indefinable element that lifts the book above the others. The date of the award is based on the date that the books were published, not when the award is announced. Administered by: CILIP, 7 Ridgmount Street, London WC1E 7AE, tel: 020 7255 0650, fax: 020 7255 0501, email: ckg@cilip.org.uk.

2005  *Tamar* by Mal Peet (Walker)
2004  *Millions* by Frank Catterall Boyce (Macmillan)
2003  *A Gathering Light* by Jennifer Donnelly (Bloomsbury)
2002  *Ruby Holler* by Sharon Creech (Bloomsbury)

## The Kate Greenaway Medal
Annual

This award was instituted in 1955 and goes to an artist who has produced the most distinguished work in the illustration of children's books. Nominated books are assessed for design, format and production as well as artistic merit and must have been published in the UK during the previous year. Administered by: CILIP, 7 Ridgmount Street, London WC1E 7AE, tel: 020 7255 0650, fax: 020 7255 0501, email: ckg@cilip.org.uk.

2005  Emily Gravett   *Wolves* (Macmillan)
2004  Chris Riddell   Jonathan Swift's *Gulliver*
                       text by Michael Jenkins (Walker)
2003  Shirley Hughes  *Ella's Big Chance* (Bodley Head)
2002  Bob Graham      *Jethro Byrde, Fairy Child* (Bodley Head)

## Children's Laureate
Biennial

The Children's Laureate is chosen every two years and is somebody who writes or illustrates books that young people love. Their books are the kind that you'll never give away, books you'll remember for the rest of your life. The Children's Laureate is a working prize intended to provide a platform for the winner to stimulate public discussion about the importance of children's literature and reading in a forward looking society.

2005  Jaqueline Wilson      2001  Anne Fine
2003  Michael Morpurgo      1999  Quentin Blake

## Costa Children's Book of the Year Award — Annual

(formerly Whitbread)

The Whitbread awards started in 1971 and the first award for a children's novel was given in 1972. The format changed in 1985 when the Whitbread Book of the Year was launched, and in 1996, children's books were taken out of the main category and given a prize of their own. Costa took over the award in 2006. Entries must be by authors who have been resident in the UK or Eire for three years and whose book has been published between 1 November and 31 October of the year of the prize. The prize is £5,000. The winner is announced in January. 1999 was the first year the winner of the Whitbread Children's Book of the Year Award was also considered for the overall Whitbread Book of the Year Award, with a prize of £25,000. Main contact: Anne O'Keane, The Bookseller's Association, Minster Road, 272 Vauxhall Bridge, London SW1V 1BA, tel: 020 7802 0801, email: anne.okeane@bookseller.org.uk.

2006 *Set in Stone* by Linda Newbery (David Fickling)

2005 *The New Policeman* by Kate Thompson (Bodley Head)

2004 *Not the End of the World* by Geraldine McCaughrean (Oxford University Press)

2003 *The Fire-Eaters* by David Almond (Hodder)

## Guardian Children's Fiction Award — Annual

The prize of £1,500 is awarded to an outstanding work of fiction for children (not picture books) written by a British or Commonwealth author and first published in the UK during the calendar year preceding the year in which the award is presented. Following publisher entry only, the winner is chosen by a panel of authors and the review editor for The Guardian's Children's Books section. For more information contact: The Guardian Newspaper, 119 Farringdon Road, London EC1R 3ER, tel: 020 7239 9694 or fax: 020 8713 4366.

2006 *A Darkling Plain* by Philip Reeve (Scholastic)

2005 *The New Policeman* by Kate Thompson (Doubleday)

2004 *How I Live Now* by Meg Rosoff (Puffin)

2003 *The Curious Incident of the Dog in the Night* by Mark Haddon (Cape/David Fickling)

**Prizes**

## NASEN/TES Book Award

This award is sponsored by the National Association for Special Educational Needs and the TES. The award, a prize of £500, is given to the book of any genre that most successfully provides a positive image of children or young people with special needs. The judges look for books that are well written and well presented and which can be appreciated by all children under the age of 16, not just those with special needs. Administration contact: Kerry Paige, The NASEN & TES Book Awards, Admiral House, 66-68 East Smithfield, London E1W 1BX Tel: 020 7782 3403 email: kerry.paige@newsint.co.uk.

2006 **Looking after Louis** by Lesley Ely illus. by Polly Dunbar (Frances Lincoln Children's Books )

2005 **Caged in Chaos** by Victoria Biggs (Jessica Kingsley)

2004 **Al Capone Does My Shirts** by Gennifer Choldenko (Bloomsbury)

2003 **Freaks, Geeks and Asperger's Syndrome** by Luke Jackson (Jessica Kingsley)

## Nestlé Children's Book Prize

The Nestlé Book Prize (formerly the Nestlé Smarties Book Prize) was established to encourage high standards and stimulate interest in books for children. Awarded annually to a work of fiction or poetry for children. Gold, Silver and Bronze awards are given in each of three categories: 5 and under, 6 to 8 and 9 to 11 years. Since 1996, the winners have been selected by young judges from a short-list drawn up by adult judges. For enquiries about the prize please contact: Booktrust, Book House, 45 East Hill, London SW18 2QZ, tel: 020 8516 2972, email: hannah@booktrust.co.uk.

### Gold Awards

2006 9-11 **The Diamond of Drury Lane** by Julia Golding (Egmont)

6-8 **Mouse Noses on Toast** by Daren King (Faber)

5 & under **That Rabbit Belongs to Emily Brown** by Cressida Cowell & Neal Layton (Orchard)

2005 9-11 **I, Coriander** by Sally Gardener (Orion)

6-8 **The Whisperer** by Nick Butterworth (HarperCollins)

5 & under **Lost and Found** by Oliver Jeffers (HarperCollins)

2004 9-11 **Spilled Water** by Sally Grindley (Bloomsbury)

6-8 **Fergus Crane** by Paul Stewart & Chris Riddell (Doubleday)

5 & under **Biscuit Bear** by Mini Grey (Cape)

2003 9-11 **The Fire-Eaters** by David Almond (Hodder)

6-8 **Varjek Paw** by S F Said (David Fickling)

5 & under **The Witch's Children & the Queen** by Ursula Jones illus. by Russell Ayto (Orchard)

## North East Book Award Annual

Initiated in 1999, this prize is awarded to a book written by an author resident in the UK and first published in paperback. A shortlist of five titles is selected by local librarians and teachers in conjunction with Northumberland Schools Library Service and the final winner is chosen by Year 10 pupils from participating schools. For more information contact: Eileen Armstrong, Cramlington High School, Cramlington, Northumberland NE23 6BN, tel: 01670 712 311, fax: 01670 730 598.

2006  *The Foreshadowing* by Marcus Sedgwick (Orion)

2005  *Looking for JJ* by Anne Cassidy (Scholastic)
    *Roxy's Baby* by Catherine MacPhail (Bloomsbury)

2004  *Lucas* by Kevin Brooks (The Chicken House)

2003  *Blinded by the Light* by Sherry Ashworth (Collins)


## Red House Children's Book Award Annual

The only major book prize in the UK decided by the readers. The award is made annually to the best work of fiction for children after hundreds of books have been read, digested and voted for, by children. The federation of Children's Book Groups co-ordinates the award, acting as an umbrella organisation for autonomous book groups across the UK. Children from within these book groups carry out initial reviewing, and eventually chosing a shortlist of ten titles that all children can vote on. As well as deciding who the overall winner will be the votes cast determine three other categories: Book for Younger Children, Book for Younger Readers and Book for Older Readers. Contact: Philippa Perry tel: 02072479695, email: pnlp@dircon.co.uk.

2006  Book for Younger Children
    *Pigs Might Fly* by Jonathan Emmett & Steve Cox (Puffin)
    Book for Younger Readers
    *Spy Dog* by Andrew Cope (Puffin)
    Book for Older Readers & **Overall Winner**
    *Percy Jackson & the Olympians: Lightning Thief* by Rick Riordan (Puffin)

2005  Book for Younger Children & **Overall Winner**
    *Baby Brains* by Simon James (Walker)
    Book for Younger Readers
    *Best Friends* by Jaqueline Wilson (Doubleday)
    Book for Older Readers
    *The Recruit* by Robert Muchamore (Hodder)

2004    Book for Younger Children
*Billy's Bucket* by Kes Gray (Bodley Head)
Book for Younger Readers
*The Mum Hunt* by Gwyneth Rees (Macmillan)
Book for Older Readers & **Overall Winner**
*Private Peaceful* by Michael Morpurgo (HarperCollins)

2003    Book for Younger Children
*Pants* by Giles Andreae & Nick Sharratt (David Fickling)
Book for Younger Readers
*Blitzed* by Robert Swindells (Doubleday)
Book for Older Readers & **Overall Winner**
*Skeleton Key* by Anthony Horowitz (Walker)

## Sheffield Children's Book Award    Annual

The Sheffield Children's Book Award began in 1989 and is presented annually to the book chosen as the most enjoyable by the children of Sheffield. The majority of the judges look at, read and vote on the shortlisted books within their class at school. There are three category winners and an overall winner. For further details contact: Jennifer Wilson (Book Award Co-ordinator), c/o Schools Library Service Sheffield, tel: 0114 250 6843, email: jennifer.wilson@sheffield.gov.uk

2006    Picture Book
*Letterbox Lil - a Cautionary Tale* by Jim Helmore
illus. by Karen Wall (Oxford University Press)
Shorter Novel & **2006 Overall Winner**
*The Amazing Story of Adolphus Tipps* by Michael Morpurgo
illus. by Michael Foreman (HarperCollins)
Longer Novel
*Elsewhere* by Gabrielle Zevin (Bloomsbury)

2005    Picture Book
*Spookrumpus* by Tony Mitton illus. by Guy Parker Rees (Orchard)
Shorter Novel
*Avenger* by Pete Johnson illus. by David Wyatt (Corgi Yearling)
Longer Novel & **2005 Overall Winner**
*Looking for JJ* by Anne Cassidy (Scholastic)

2004 Picture Book
  *Jennifer Jones Won't Leave me Alone* by Frieda Wishinsky and
    Neal Layton (Doubleday)
  Shorter Novel
  *Mokee Joe is Coming* by Peter J Murray (Pen Press & Hodder)
  Longer Novel & **2004 Overall Winner**
  *The Curious Incident of the Dog in the Night-time* by Mark Haddon
    (Red Fox)
2003 Picture Book
  *Snow Bear* by Piers Harper (Macmillan Children's Books)
  Shorter Novel & **2003 Overall Winner**
  *Molly Moon's Incredible Book of Hypnotism* by Georgia Byng
    (Macmillan Children's Books)
  Longer Novel
  *Child X* by Lee Weatherly (Corgi)

## Tir na n-Og Award Annual

The Tir na n-Og Awards are three prizes of £1,000 awarded annually to
acknowledge the work of authors and illustrators in three categories.
These are Best Fiction of the Year (original Welsh-language novels,
stories and picture-books are considered); Best Welsh-Language
Non-fiction Book of the Year; and Best English (Anglo-Welsh) Book of
the Year (with an authentic Welsh background, fiction and non-fiction).
Books must be published during the preceding year. For more details,
contact the Administrators: Welsh Books Council, Castell Brychan,
Aberystwyth SY23 2JB, tel: 01970 624 151 or fax: 01970 625 385,
email: castellbrychan@cllc.org.uk, website: www.cllc.org.uk.

2006 Best Welsh fiction (Primary sector)
  *Carreg Ateb* by Emily Huws (Cymdeithas Lyfrrau Ceridigion)
  Best Welsh fiction (Secondary sector)
  *Creadyn* by Gwion Hallam (Gwasg Gomer)
  Best English fiction
  *Tirion's Secret Journal* by Jenny Sullivan (Pont Books)
2005 Best Welsh fiction
  *Eco* by Emily Huws (Cymdeithas Lyfrrau Ceridigion)
  Best Welsh non-fiction
  *Byd Llawn Hud* by Mererid Hopwood (Gwasg Gomer)
  Best English fiction
  *The Seal Children* by Jackie Morris (Frances Lincoln)

**Prizes**

## Tir na n-Og Award (cont) Annual

2004 Best Welsh fiction
*Iawn Boi?* by Caryl Lewis (Y Lolfa)
Best Welsh non-fiction
*Stori Dafydd ap Gwilym* by Gyn Thomas & Margaret Jones (Y Lolfa)
Best English fiction
*The Battle of Mametz Woods, 1916* by Robert Phillips (CAA)

2003 Best Welsh fiction
*Sgôr* by Bethan Gwanas (Y Lolfa)
Best Welsh non-fiction
*Dewi Sant* by Rhiannon Ifans & Margaret Jones (Y Lolfa)
Best English fiction
*Cold Jac* by Rob Lewis (Gomer/Pont)

## Wirral Paperback of the Year Annual

Set up in 1995, this award is organised by the Wirral Schools Library Service. It aims to give young people from the area the chance to read exciting new fiction. The Schools Library Service chooses 20 titles, first published in paperback in the preceding year. Copies are lent to up to 20 local secondary schools. Year 8 and 9 pupils from each school choose their own shortlist and a Wirral shortlist is then compiled from these in May. Representatives from each school meet in July to discuss and vote for their favourite book. For further information contact: Mary Bryning, Wirral Schools Library Service, Wirral Education Centre, Acre Lane, Bromborough, Wirral CH62 7BZ, tel: 0151 346 1184, email: sls@wirral.gov.uk.

2006 *Looking for JJ* by Anne Cassidy (Scholastic)
2005 *The Curious Incident of the Dog in the Night-time* by Mark Haddon (Red Fox)
2004 *Across the Nightingale Floor* by Lian Hearn (Picador)
2003 *Noughts and Crosses* by Malorie Blackman (Corgi)

# Exploring Further and Keeping up to Date

## Books

*Oxford Companion to Children's Literature*                    1999
Edited by Humphrey Carpenter and Mari Prichard
ISBN 0 19 860228 6
Oxford University Press

*The Cambridge Guide to Children's Books in English*          2001
Edited by Victor Watson
ISBN 0 521 55064 5
Cambridge University Press

*Twentieth Century Children's Writers*                    3rd ed 1989
ISBN 0 912289 95 3
St James Press (USA)

*The Rough Guide to Children's Books 0–5 Years*               2002
Nicholas Tucker
ISBN 1 85828 787 1
Rough Guides

*The Rough Guide to Children's Books 5–11 Years*             2002
Nicholas Tucker
ISBN 1 85828 788 X
Rough Guides

*The Rough Guide to Books for Teenagers*                     2003
Nicholas Tucker & Julia Eccleshare
ISBN 1 84353 138 0
Rough Guides

*Children's Literature*                                       2001
Peter Hunt
ISBN 0 631 21141 1
Blackwell

*Son of Invisible Art: Graphic Novels for Libraries*         2001
Compiled by Joss O'Kelly
ISBN 0 86059 605 2
Buckinghamshire County Library

## Books (cont)

**Simply the Best Books for Children**      2003
Books for 0 to 7 years
Ann Lazim & Sue Ellis (ed Myra Barrs)
ISBN 1 872267 32 7
Centre for Literacy in Primary Education (CLPE)

**Simply the Best Books for Children**      2003
Books for 7 to 11 years
Ann Lazim & Sue Ellis (ed Myra Barrs)
Centre for Literacy in Primary Education (CLPE)

**Great Books to Read Aloud**      2006
Jacqueline Wilson
ISBN 0 552 55498 7
Corgi

**Riveting Reads 6–8**      2006
Prue Goodwin
ISBN 978190344635 5
School Library Association

**Riveting Reads 8–12**      2006
Jo Sennitt
ISBN 1903446309
School Library Association

**Riveting Reads 12–16**      2006
Eileen Armstrong
ISBN 1 903 446325
School Library Association

**Riveting Reads Plus: a View of the World**      2006
Oxford Branch of the School Library Association
School Library Association

**Boys and Girls Forever: Children's Classics**      2003
**from Cinderella to Harry Potter**
Alison Lurie
ISBN 014 2002526
Penguin

## Books (cont)

*Modern Children's Literature: an Introduction*     2004
Kimberley Reynolds
ISBN 1403916128
Palgrave

*The Ultimate Book Guide: Over 600 Top Books for 8–12s*    2004
Daniel Hahn, Leonie Flynn & Susan Reuben (Eds)
ISBN 0173667184
A & C Black

*The Ultimate Teen Book Guide*     2006
Daniel Hahn & Leonie Flynn (Eds)
ISBN 0713673303
A & C Black

## Periodicals

*Books for Keeps: The Children's Book Magazine*
Books for Keeps
1 Effingham Road
London SE12 8NZ
Phone: 020 8852 4953
E-mail: enquiries@booksforkeeps.co.uk
Six issues per year

*Carousel: The Guide to Children's Books*
Carousel
The Saturn Centre
54–76 Bissell Street
Birmingham B5 7HX
Phone: 0121 622 7458
E-mail: enquiries@carouselguide.co.uk
Three issues per year plus Christmas supplement

*The School Librarian*
Unit 2
Lotmead Business Village
Lotmead Farm
Wanborough
Swindon
Phone: 01793 791787
E-mail: publications@sla.org.uk
Four issues per year

Exploring further

## Websites

Websites are a good way of exploring the world of children's literature. These days many authors and illustrators have their own website and it is always worth putting a name into a search engine to see if a site will come up. Many are hosted on publishers' sites or signposted from information or library sites. The sites listed below are helpful but please note that although they were accurate at the time of going to press, they may change during the life of this edition.

www.achuka.co.uk
News and views about children's books. Information on authors and illustrators.

www.bbc.co.uk
Links to Jackanory, Blue Peter etc. Follow-ups on books appearing on programmes. Games and things to do.

www.bookheads.org.uk
Site for teenagers developed from Booktrust to promote teenage reading in conjunction with its Teenage Book Prize.

http://books.guardian.co.uk
Children's Library section of main website. Suggestions for building a child's library. News, reviews.

www.booktrusted.com
Booktrust is an educational charity which hosts this comprehensive site for people wanting to find out more about books for all ages.

www.channel4.com/learning/microsites/B/bookbox/home.htm
Information on popular authors, illustrators and books.

www.clpe.co.uk
Site of the Centre for Literacy in Primary Education. Aimed at teachers but useful for all interested in children's books and reading.

www.cool-reads.co.uk
Reviews for and by 10–15 year olds.

www.enjoyengland.com/storybook
Site relates books to actual locations in England. Gives information on book background localities. Links to tourist boards encouraging people to visit.

www.fcbg.org.uk
Federation of Children's Book Groups site. A network of book groups founded by parents to further the love of books and reading. Has a useful list of links to topics of interest.

www.kidsatrandomhouse.co.uk
News about latest books. Links to authors/illustrators. Interactive book chooser. Fun and games.

www.kidsreview.org.uk
Site aims to help locate appropriate books. Can be used to link with schools, enabling children to use it from home and school. Can be used to purchase books.

www.literacytrust.org.uk
News and views on books and reading. Reports on initiatives. Of interest to anyone involved in children's books. Signposting to areas of interest including an area on websites about children's books and reading.

www.mrsmad.com
For children of all ages plus teachers, parents & librarians. Reviews, lists games and stories.

www.ncll.org.uk
Site of the National Centre for Language and Literacy at Reading University. Great resource for teachers and librarians. Resources, news on events, how to find authors for events.

www.readingmatters.co.uk
Reviews. Also book chooser – a series of questions are asked about what to read – a selection of titles offered as a result.

www.rif.org.uk
Reading is Fundamental is an initiative of the National Literacy Trust that promotes reading for fun and the importance of books for children.

www.ukchildrensbooks.co.uk
Directory of authors, illustrators, publishers, organisations.

www.wordpool.co.uk
Site for parents, teachers, writers and children. Links to author/illustrator sites. Information and tips for aspiring writers.

Exploring further

171

# Index

| Author | Age ranges | Page numbers |
|--------|-----------|--------------|
| Abela, Deborah | 8-11 | 33 |
| Adams, Richard | 8-11 | 33 |
| Adeney, Anne | 5-7 | 1 |
| Ahlberg, Allan | 5-7  8-11 | 1, 33 |
| Aiken, Joan | 8-11  12-14 | 33, 91 |
| Alcott, Louisa May | 8-11 | 33 |
| Alexander, Lloyd | 12-14 | 91 |
| Allen, Jonathan | 5-7 | 1 |
| Allen-Gray, Alison | 12-14 | 91 |
| Almond, David | 8-11  12-14 | 34, 91 |
| Anderson, Rachel | 8-11  12-14 | 34, 91 |
| Anderson, Scoular | 5-7 | 1 |
| Andreae, Giles | 5-7  8-11 | 2, 34 |
| Anholt, Laurence | 5-7  8-11 | 2, 35 |
| Apps, Roy | 5-7  8-11 | 2, 34 |
| Ardagh, Philip | 8-11 | 35 |
| Arkle, Phyllis | 5-7 | 2 |
| Arksey, Neil | 8-11 | 35 |
| Arnold, Louise | 8-11 | 35 |
| Arrigan, Mary | 8-11 | 35 |
| Ashley, Bernard | 12-14 | 92 |
| Ashworth, Sherry | 12-14 | 92 |
| Asquith, Ros | 8-11  12-14 | 35, 92 |
| Augarde, Steve | 8-11 | 36 |
| Bajoria, Paul | 8-11 | 36 |
| Baker, E D | 8-11 | 36 |
| Baldry, Cherith | 8-11 | 36 |
| Balliett, Blue | 8-11 | 36 |
| Banks, Lynne Reid | 8-11  12-14 | 36, 92 |
| Barber, Antonia | 5-7  8-11 | 2, 37 |
| Barker, Dominic | 8-11  12-14 | 37, 92 |
| Barker, Raffaella | 12-14 | 92 |
| Barlow and Steve Skidmore, Steve | 8-11 | 37 |
| Barrie, J M | 8-11 | 37 |
| Bartram, Simon | 5-7 | 3 |
| Bates, Michelle | 8-11 | 37 |
| Bauer, Joan | 12-14 | 93 |
| Baum, Frank L | 8-11 | 37 |
| Bawden, Nina | 8-11 | 38 |
| Beardsley, Martyn | 5-7  8-11 | 3, 38 |
| Beck, Ian | 8-11 | 38 |
| Bedford, David | 8-11 | 38 |
| Belbin, David | 12-14 | 93 |
| Bennett, Veronica | 12-14 | 93 |
| Berenstain, Stan and Jan | 5-7 | 3 |

Bertagna, Julie    8-11   12-14 .......................... 38, 93
Besson, Luc    8-11 ........................................ 38
Birdsall, Jeanne    8-11 ................................... 39
Black, Holly    8-11   12-14 ............................ 39, 93
Blacker, Terence    5-7   8-11   12-14 ............... 3, 39, 94
Blackford, Andy    5-7 ...................................... 3
Blackman, Malorie    5-7   8-11   12-14 ............ 4, 39, 94
Blake, Jon    5-7 .......................................... 4
Blathwayt, Benedict    5-7 ................................. 4
Bloor, Thomas    8-11 ..................................... 39
Blume, Judy    8-11 ....................................... 40
Blyton, Enid    8-11 ...................................... 40
Bond, Michael    8-11 ..................................... 40
Boote, Adrian    5-7 ....................................... 4
Booth, Martin    12-14 .................................... 94
Boston, Lucy M    8-11 .................................... 40
Bowkett, Stephen    8-11   12-14 ...................... 40, 94
Bowler, Tim    12-14 ...................................... 94
Boyce, Frank Cottrell    8-11   12-14 ................. 40, 95
Boyne, John    12-14 ...................................... 95
Bradman, Tony    5-7   8-11 ............................. 4, 41
Brand, Christiana    8-11 ................................. 41
Branford, Henrietta    5-7   8-11 ....................... 4, 41
Brashares, Ann    12-14 ................................... 95
Brennan, Herbie    5-7   8-11 ........................... 5, 41
Brent-Dyer, Elinor M    8-11 .............................. 41
Breslin, Theresa    8-11   12-14 ...................... 41, 95
Briggs, Raymond    5-7   8-11 .......................... 5, 42
Brisley, Joyce Lankester    5-7 ............................ 5
Brooks, Kevin    12-14 .................................... 95
Brown, Jeff    5-7 ......................................... 5
Brown, Judy    5-7 ......................................... 5
Brown, Marc    5-7 ......................................... 5
Browne, N M    12-14 ...................................... 96
Bruce, Lisa    5-7 ......................................... 6
Brumpton, Keith    5-7 ..................................... 6
Bryant, Ann    5-7   8-11 ............................... 6, 42
Buckley-Archer, Linda    8-11 ............................. 42
Burchett and Sara Vogler, Janet    5-7 .................... 6
Burgess, Melvin    8-11   12-14 ....................... 42, 96
Burnard, Damon    5-7 ...................................... 6
Burnett, Frances Hodgson    8-11 .......................... 42
Butcher, A J    12-14 ..................................... 96
Butterworth, Nick    5-7 ................................... 7
Byars, Betsy    8-11 ...................................... 42
Byng, Georgia    8-11 ..................................... 43
Cabot, Meg    12-14 ....................................... 96
Cameron, Ann    5-7 ........................................ 7
Canavan, Trudi    12-14 ................................... 96
Cann, Kate    12-14 ....................................... 97
Carpenter, Humphrey    5-7 ................................. 7

**Index**

Carroll, Lewis  8-11 .................................................. 43
Cassidy, Anne  5-7  12-14 ........................................ 7, 97
Cassidy, Cathy  8-11  12-14 .................................. 43, 97
Castor, Harriet  5-7 ................................................... 7
Cattell, Bob  8-11 .................................................... 43
Cave, Kathryn  8-11 ................................................. 43
Cave, Patrick  12-14 ................................................. 97
Chandler, Pauline  12-14 .......................................... 97
Chapman, Linda  5-7  8-11 .................................... 8, 43
Chapman, Simon  8-11 .............................................. 44
Child, Lauren  5-7  8-11 ........................................ 8, 44
Childs, Rob  5-7  8-11 .......................................... 8, 44
Choldenko, Gennifer  12-14 ...................................... 97
Clark, Emma Chichester  5-7 ..................................... 8
Clarke, Julia  12-14 ................................................ 98
Clement-Davies, David  8-11 ..................................... 44
Clover, Peter  5-7 .................................................... 8
Coburn, Ann  12-14 ................................................. 98
Cole, Stephen  12-14 ............................................... 98
Cole, Steve  8-11 .................................................... 44
Coleman, Michael  5-7  8-11 ................................... 9, 45
Colfer, Eoin  8-11  12-14 ..................................... 45, 98
Cooper, Louise  8-11  12-14 .................................. 45, 98
Cooper, Susan  8-11  12-14 ................................... 45, 98
Cope, Andrew  5-7  8-11 ........................................ 9, 45
Coppard, Yvonne  8-11 ............................................. 46
Corbett, W J  8-11 .................................................. 46
Corder, Zizou  8-11 ................................................. 46
Coville, Bruce  8-11 ................................................ 46
Cowell, Cressida  8-11 ............................................. 46
Craig, Joe  12-14 .................................................... 99
Crebbin, June  5-7 .................................................... 9
Creech, Sharon  8-11  12-14 .................................. 47, 99
Cresswell, Helen  8-11 ............................................. 47
Croggon, Alison  12-14 ............................................ 99
Crompton, Richmal  8-11 .......................................... 47
Cronin, Michael  12-14 ............................................ 99
Cross, Gillian  8-11  12-14 .................................... 47, 99
Crossley-Holland, Kevin  8-11  12-14 ...................... 47, 100
Crowley, Bridget  8-11 ............................................. 48
Cunliffe, John  5-7 ................................................... 9
Curley, Marianne  12-14 .......................................... 100
d'Lacey, Chris  5-7  8-11 ....................................... 9, 48
Dahl, Roald  5-7  8-11 .......................................... 9, 48
Dale, Anna  8-11 .................................................... 48
Dale, Jenny  5-7  8-11 ......................................... 10, 48
Dalton, Annie  8-11 ................................................ 49
Daniels, Lucy  5-7  8-11 ...................................... 10, 49
Dann, Colin  8-11 ................................................... 49
Danziger, Paula  8-11 ............................................. 49
Deary, Terry  8-11 ............................................... 50

Delaney, Joseph    8-11   12-14   . . . . . . . . . . . . . . . . . . . . . . . . . 50, 100
Dhami, Narinder    8-11   12-14   . . . . . . . . . . . . . . . . . . . . . . . 50, 100
di Camillo, Kate    8-11   . . . . . . . . . . . . . . . . . . . . . . . . . . . . . . . 50
Dickinson, John    12-14   . . . . . . . . . . . . . . . . . . . . . . . . . . . . . .100
Dickinson, Peter    12-14   . . . . . . . . . . . . . . . . . . . . . . . . . . . . . .101
Doder, Joshua    8-11   . . . . . . . . . . . . . . . . . . . . . . . . . . . . . . . . 50
Doherty, Berlie    8-11   12-14   . . . . . . . . . . . . . . . . . . . . . . . .51, 101
Dolan, Penny    5-7   . . . . . . . . . . . . . . . . . . . . . . . . . . . . . . . . . .10
Donaldson, Julia    5-7   . . . . . . . . . . . . . . . . . . . . . . . . . . . . . . . .10
Donnelly, Jennifer    12-14   . . . . . . . . . . . . . . . . . . . . . . . . . . . . .101
Dowswell, Paul    8-11   12-14   . . . . . . . . . . . . . . . . . . . . . . . . .51, 101
Doyle, Malachy    5-7   8-11   . . . . . . . . . . . . . . . . . . . . . . . . . .11, 51
Doyle, Roddy    8-11   . . . . . . . . . . . . . . . . . . . . . . . . . . . . . . . . .51
Duey, Kathleen    8-11   . . . . . . . . . . . . . . . . . . . . . . . . . . . . . . . .51
Dunbar, Fiona    8-11   . . . . . . . . . . . . . . . . . . . . . . . . . . . . . . . . .51
Dunbar, Joyce    5-7   . . . . . . . . . . . . . . . . . . . . . . . . . . . . . . . . . 11
Dunmore, Helen    5-7   8-11   . . . . . . . . . . . . . . . . . . . . . . . . . .11, 52
DuPrau, Jeanne    8-11   . . . . . . . . . . . . . . . . . . . . . . . . . . . . . . . 52
Durant, Alan    5-7   8-11   . . . . . . . . . . . . . . . . . . . . . . . . . . . .11, 52
Dyer, Heather    8-11   . . . . . . . . . . . . . . . . . . . . . . . . . . . . . . . . 52
Eastman, P D    5-7   . . . . . . . . . . . . . . . . . . . . . . . . . . . . . . . . . . 11
Edwards, Dorothy    5-7   . . . . . . . . . . . . . . . . . . . . . . . . . . . . . . .12
Elboz, Stephen    8-11   12-14   . . . . . . . . . . . . . . . . . . . . . . . . .52, 101
Ellis, Deborah    12-14   . . . . . . . . . . . . . . . . . . . . . . . . . . . . . . . .102
Emmett, Jonathan    5-7   . . . . . . . . . . . . . . . . . . . . . . . . . . . . . . .12
Fardell, John    8-11   . . . . . . . . . . . . . . . . . . . . . . . . . . . . . . . . . 52
Farmer, Nancy    12-14   . . . . . . . . . . . . . . . . . . . . . . . . . . . . . . . .102
Fearnley, Jan    5-7   . . . . . . . . . . . . . . . . . . . . . . . . . . . . . . . . . .12
Feeney, Josephine    12-14   . . . . . . . . . . . . . . . . . . . . . . . . . . . . . .102
Fine, Anne    5-7   8-11   12-14   . . . . . . . . . . . . . . . . . . . . . 12, 53, 102
Finney, Patricia    8-11   . . . . . . . . . . . . . . . . . . . . . . . . . . . . . . . 53
Fisher, Catherine    8-11   12-14   . . . . . . . . . . . . . . . . . . . . . . . 53, 102
Flegg, Aubrey    12-14   . . . . . . . . . . . . . . . . . . . . . . . . . . . . . . . .103
Fletcher, Charlie    8-11   12-14   . . . . . . . . . . . . . . . . . . . . . . . 53, 103
Forde, Catherine    12-14   . . . . . . . . . . . . . . . . . . . . . . . . . . . . . . .103
French, Jackie    8-11   . . . . . . . . . . . . . . . . . . . . . . . . . . . . . . . . 53
French, Vivian    5-7   . . . . . . . . . . . . . . . . . . . . . . . . . . . . . . . . .12
Friel, Maeve    5-7   8-11   . . . . . . . . . . . . . . . . . . . . . . . . . . . 13, 54
Funke, Cornelia    8-11   . . . . . . . . . . . . . . . . . . . . . . . . . . . . . . . 54
Gaiman, Neil    5-7   8-11   . . . . . . . . . . . . . . . . . . . . . . . . . . . 13, 54
Gantos, Jack    8-11   . . . . . . . . . . . . . . . . . . . . . . . . . . . . . . . . . 54
Gardner, Graham    12-14   . . . . . . . . . . . . . . . . . . . . . . . . . . . . . .103
Gardner, Sally    5-7   8-11   12-14   . . . . . . . . . . . . . . . . . . 13, 54, 103
Garner, Alan    8-11   . . . . . . . . . . . . . . . . . . . . . . . . . . . . . . . . . 55
Gates, Susan    8-11   12-14   . . . . . . . . . . . . . . . . . . . . . . . . . 55, 103
Gavin, Jamila    5-7   8-11   12-14   . . . . . . . . . . . . . . . . . . 13, 55, 104
Gebler, Carlo    12-14   . . . . . . . . . . . . . . . . . . . . . . . . . . . . . . . .104
Geras, Adèle    5-7   8-11   12-14   . . . . . . . . . . . . . . . . . . 13, 55, 104
Gibbons, Alan    8-11   12-14   . . . . . . . . . . . . . . . . . . . . . . . . 55, 104
Gifford, Griselda    8-11   . . . . . . . . . . . . . . . . . . . . . . . . . . . . . . . 56
Gifford, Nick    12-14   . . . . . . . . . . . . . . . . . . . . . . . . . . . . . . . .104

Index

Gleitzman, Morris   8-11   12-14 . . . . . . . . . . . . . . . . . . . . . . . 56, 105
Gliori, Debi   8-11 . . . . . . . . . . . . . . . . . . . . . . . . . . . . . . . . . . 56
Glover, Sandra   8-11   12-14 . . . . . . . . . . . . . . . . . . . . . . . 56, 105
Golding, Julia   8-11 . . . . . . . . . . . . . . . . . . . . . . . . . . . . . . . 56
Goodhart, Pippa   5-7   8-11 . . . . . . . . . . . . . . . . . . . . . . . 14, 57
Gordon, John   8-11 . . . . . . . . . . . . . . . . . . . . . . . . . . . . . . . . 57
Goscinny, René   8-11 . . . . . . . . . . . . . . . . . . . . . . . . . . . . . . 57
Goswell, Simon   8-11 . . . . . . . . . . . . . . . . . . . . . . . . . . . . . . 57
Goudge, Elizabeth   8-11 . . . . . . . . . . . . . . . . . . . . . . . . . . . . 57
Grahame, Kenneth   8-11 . . . . . . . . . . . . . . . . . . . . . . . . . . . . 57
Grant, John   5-7 . . . . . . . . . . . . . . . . . . . . . . . . . . . . . . . . . .14
Graves, Sue   5-7 . . . . . . . . . . . . . . . . . . . . . . . . . . . . . . . . . .14
Gravett, Emily   5-7 . . . . . . . . . . . . . . . . . . . . . . . . . . . . . . . .14
Gray, Keith   12-14 . . . . . . . . . . . . . . . . . . . . . . . . . . . . . . . .105
Gray, Kes   5-7   8-11 . . . . . . . . . . . . . . . . . . . . . . . . . . . . 14, 58
Green, Julia   12-14 . . . . . . . . . . . . . . . . . . . . . . . . . . . . . . .105
Grey, Mini   5-7 . . . . . . . . . . . . . . . . . . . . . . . . . . . . . . . . . . .15
Griffiths, Andy   8-11 . . . . . . . . . . . . . . . . . . . . . . . . . . . . . . 58
Grindley, Sally   5-7   8-11 . . . . . . . . . . . . . . . . . . . . . . . . 15, 58
Groening, Matt   12-14 . . . . . . . . . . . . . . . . . . . . . . . . . . . . .105
Gross, Philip   12-14 . . . . . . . . . . . . . . . . . . . . . . . . . . . . . . .105
Gutteridge, Alex   5-7 . . . . . . . . . . . . . . . . . . . . . . . . . . . . . .15
Haddon, Mark   8-11   12-14 . . . . . . . . . . . . . . . . . . . . . . . 58, 106
Halam, Ann   12-14 . . . . . . . . . . . . . . . . . . . . . . . . . . . . . . .106
Hale, Shannon   12-14 . . . . . . . . . . . . . . . . . . . . . . . . . . . . .106
Hamley, Dennis   5-7   8-11 . . . . . . . . . . . . . . . . . . . . . . . 15, 58
Hanley, Victoria   12-14 . . . . . . . . . . . . . . . . . . . . . . . . . . . .106
Hanson, Dave   5-7 . . . . . . . . . . . . . . . . . . . . . . . . . . . . . . .15
Hardinge, Frances   12-14 . . . . . . . . . . . . . . . . . . . . . . . . . . .106
Harper, Meg   8-11 . . . . . . . . . . . . . . . . . . . . . . . . . . . . . . . 58
Hartnett, Sonya   12-14 . . . . . . . . . . . . . . . . . . . . . . . . . . . .106
Harvey, Damian   5-7 . . . . . . . . . . . . . . . . . . . . . . . . . . . . . .16
Hearn, Julie   12-14 . . . . . . . . . . . . . . . . . . . . . . . . . . . . . . .106
Hearn, Lian   12-14 . . . . . . . . . . . . . . . . . . . . . . . . . . . . . . .107
Hedges, Carol   8-11 . . . . . . . . . . . . . . . . . . . . . . . . . . . . . . 59
Henderson, Kathy   5-7 . . . . . . . . . . . . . . . . . . . . . . . . . . . . .16
Hendry, Diana   8-11 . . . . . . . . . . . . . . . . . . . . . . . . . . . . . . 59
Hendry, Frances Mary   12-14 . . . . . . . . . . . . . . . . . . . . . . .107
Hergé,   8-11 . . . . . . . . . . . . . . . . . . . . . . . . . . . . . . . . . . 59
Hiaasen, Carl   12-14 . . . . . . . . . . . . . . . . . . . . . . . . . . . . .107
Hiçyilmaz, Gaye   12-14 . . . . . . . . . . . . . . . . . . . . . . . . . . . .107
Hightman, Jason   8-11 . . . . . . . . . . . . . . . . . . . . . . . . . . . . 59
Higson, Charlie   8-11   12-14 . . . . . . . . . . . . . . . . . . . . . . 59, 107
Hill, Stuart   12-14 . . . . . . . . . . . . . . . . . . . . . . . . . . . . . . .107
Hinton, Nigel   8-11   12-14 . . . . . . . . . . . . . . . . . . . . . . . 59, 108
Hinton, S E   12-14 . . . . . . . . . . . . . . . . . . . . . . . . . . . . . . .108
Hoeye, Michael   8-11 . . . . . . . . . . . . . . . . . . . . . . . . . . . . . 60
Hoffman, Mary   5-7   12-14 . . . . . . . . . . . . . . . . . . . . . . .16, 108
Holm, Anne   8-11 . . . . . . . . . . . . . . . . . . . . . . . . . . . . . . . 60
Hooper, Mary   5-7   8-11   12-14 . . . . . . . . . . . . . . . . 16, 60, 108
Hopkins, Cathy   12-14 . . . . . . . . . . . . . . . . . . . . . . . . . . . . .108

**Index**

Horowitz, Anthony    8-11   12-14   .......................60, 109
Horse, Harry    8-11   ........................................ 60
Howarth, Lesley    8-11   12-14   ........................61 109
Hughes, Shirley    5-7   .....................................16
Hughes, Ted    8-11   .......................................61
Hutton, Sam    12-14   .....................................109
Ibbotson, Eva    8-11   12-14   ........................61, 109
Ikumi, Mia    8-11   .........................................61
Impey, Rose    5-7   8-11   ...........................17, 61
Jackson and Ian Livingstone, Steve    8-11   ................ 62
Jacques, Brian    8-11   12-14   ........................62, 109
Jarman, Julia    5-7   8-11   ............................17, 62
Jarvis, Robin    8-11   12-14   ..........................62, 110
Jeapes, Ben    12-14   .....................................110
Jefferies, Cindy    8-11   ................................. 62
Jeffers, Oliver    5-7   .....................................17
Jennings, Paul    8-11   12-14   ........................63, 110
Jeram, Anita    5-7   .......................................17
Johnson, Pete    8-11   12-14   .........................63, 110
Jones, Allan Frewin    8-11   ............................... 63
Jones, Diana Wynne    8-11   12-14   ...................63, 110
Jubert, Hervé    12-14   ...................................111
Juby, Susan    12-14   .....................................111
Jungman, Ann    5-7   .......................................17
Kavanagh, Peter    5-7   ....................................18
Kay, Elizabeth    8-11   ................................... 63
Keaney, Brian    12-14   ...................................111
Kemp, Gene    8-11   ...................................... 64
Kendal, Penny    12-14   ...................................111
Kennemore, Tim    8-11   .................................. 64
Kent, Deborah    8-11   .................................... 64
Kerr, Judith    8-11   ...................................... 64
Kerr, P B    8-11   ......................................... 64
Kilworth, Garry    8-11   ................................... 64
Kimmel, Elizabeth Cody    8-11   ........................... 65
Kimpton, Diana    5-7   .....................................18
King, Clive    8-11   ....................................... 65
King-Smith, Dick    5-7   8-11   .......................18, 65
Knapman, Timothy    5-7   ..................................18
Krailing, Tessa    5-7   .....................................18
L'Homme, Erik    12-14   ................................. 111
Laird, Elizabeth    8-11   12-14   ........................65, 111
Lamb, Kathryn    12-14   ...................................112
Langrish, Katherine    8-11   ............................. 65
Larson, Hope    12-14   .....................................112
Lassiter, Rhiannon    12-14   ...............................112
Law, Karina    5-7   .........................................19
Lawrence, Caroline    8-11   ............................... 66
Lawrence, Michael    8-11   12-14   ....................66, 112
Le Guin, Ursula    12-14   ..................................112
Le Sieg, Theo    5-7   ......................................19

Lee, Tanith   12-14   . . . . . . . . . . . . . . . . . . . . . . . . . . . . . . . .113
Leonard, Elmore   8-11   . . . . . . . . . . . . . . . . . . . . . . . . . . . . . 66
Lewis, C S   8-11   . . . . . . . . . . . . . . . . . . . . . . . . . . . . . . . . . 66
Limb, Sue   12-14   . . . . . . . . . . . . . . . . . . . . . . . . . . . . . . . . .113
Lindsay, Elizabeth   5-7   8-11   . . . . . . . . . . . . . . . . . . . . . . . . 19, 66
Lingard, Joan   5-7   12-14   . . . . . . . . . . . . . . . . . . . . . . . . . .19, 113
Lively, Penelope   8-11   . . . . . . . . . . . . . . . . . . . . . . . . . . . . . 67
Llewellyn, Sam   8-11   . . . . . . . . . . . . . . . . . . . . . . . . . . . . . . 67
Lobel, Arnold   5-7   . . . . . . . . . . . . . . . . . . . . . . . . . . . . . . . .19
McBratney, Sam   5-7   . . . . . . . . . . . . . . . . . . . . . . . . . . . . . . 20
McCaughrean, Geraldine   5-7   8-11   12-14   . . . . . . . . . . 20, 67, 113
McCombie, Karen   8-11   12-14   . . . . . . . . . . . . . . . . . . . . . .67, 113
McCorkle, Mark   8-11   . . . . . . . . . . . . . . . . . . . . . . . . . . . . . 67
McDonald, Megan   5-7   8-11   . . . . . . . . . . . . . . . . . . . . . . . 20, 68
McGowan, Anthony   12-14   . . . . . . . . . . . . . . . . . . . . . . . . . .114
McKain, Kelly   5-7   8-11   . . . . . . . . . . . . . . . . . . . . . . . . . . 20, 68
McKay, Hilary   5-7   8-11   12-14   . . . . . . . . . . . . . . . . 20, 68, 114
McLaughlin, Marilyn   5-7   . . . . . . . . . . . . . . . . . . . . . . . . . . . .21
McNab and Robert Rigby, Andy   12-14   . . . . . . . . . . . . . . . . . . .114
McNaughton, Colin   5-7   . . . . . . . . . . . . . . . . . . . . . . . . . . . . .21
McNish, Cliff   12-14   . . . . . . . . . . . . . . . . . . . . . . . . . . . . . .114
MacPhail, Catherine   8-11   12-14   . . . . . . . . . . . . . . . . . . . .68, 114
Magorian, Michelle   8-11   12-14   . . . . . . . . . . . . . . . . . . . . .68, 115
Mah, Adeline Yen   12-14   . . . . . . . . . . . . . . . . . . . . . . . . . . .115
Mahy, Margaret   8-11   12-14   . . . . . . . . . . . . . . . . . . . . . . .69, 115
Mankell, Henning   12-14   . . . . . . . . . . . . . . . . . . . . . . . . . . .115
Mark, Jan   8-11   12-14   . . . . . . . . . . . . . . . . . . . . . . . . . . .69, 115
Marks, Graham   12-14   . . . . . . . . . . . . . . . . . . . . . . . . . . . .115
Marshall, Hazel   8-11   . . . . . . . . . . . . . . . . . . . . . . . . . . . . . 69
Marshall, James   5-7   . . . . . . . . . . . . . . . . . . . . . . . . . . . . . .21
Marshall, Jill   8-11   . . . . . . . . . . . . . . . . . . . . . . . . . . . . . . . 69
Mason, Simon   8-11   . . . . . . . . . . . . . . . . . . . . . . . . . . . . . . 69
Masters, Anthony   5-7   8-11   12-14   . . . . . . . . . . . . . . .21, 70, 116
Matthews, Andrew   12-14   . . . . . . . . . . . . . . . . . . . . . . . . . .116
Mayfield, Sue   12-14   . . . . . . . . . . . . . . . . . . . . . . . . . . . . .116
Mayo, Margaret   5-7   . . . . . . . . . . . . . . . . . . . . . . . . . . . . . .21
Meadows, Daisy   5-7   8-11   . . . . . . . . . . . . . . . . . . . . . . . . 22, 70
Mendes, Valerie   12-14   . . . . . . . . . . . . . . . . . . . . . . . . . . . .116
Meyer, Carolyn   12-14   . . . . . . . . . . . . . . . . . . . . . . . . . . . .116
Meyer, Kai   12-14   . . . . . . . . . . . . . . . . . . . . . . . . . . . . . . .116
Michael, Livi   8-11   . . . . . . . . . . . . . . . . . . . . . . . . . . . . . . 70
Milne, A A   8-11   . . . . . . . . . . . . . . . . . . . . . . . . . . . . . . . . 70
Mitchelhill, Barbara   5-7   8-11   . . . . . . . . . . . . . . . . . . . . . . 22, 70
Mitton, Tony   5-7   . . . . . . . . . . . . . . . . . . . . . . . . . . . . . . . 22
Molloy, Michael   8-11   12-14   . . . . . . . . . . . . . . . . . . . . . . .71, 117
Montgomery, L M   8-11   . . . . . . . . . . . . . . . . . . . . . . . . . . . .71
Moon, Nicola   5-7   . . . . . . . . . . . . . . . . . . . . . . . . . . . . . . . 22
Mooney, Bel   5-7   . . . . . . . . . . . . . . . . . . . . . . . . . . . . . . . 22
Moore, Maggie   5-7   . . . . . . . . . . . . . . . . . . . . . . . . . . . . . . 23
Morgan, Nicola   12-14   . . . . . . . . . . . . . . . . . . . . . . . . . . . .117
Morpurgo, Michael   5-7   8-11   12-14   . . . . . . . . . . . . . . .23, 71, 117

Morris, Gerald    8-11 . . . . . . . . . . . . . . . . . . . . . . . . . . . . . . . . . .71
Moss, Alexandra    8-11 . . . . . . . . . . . . . . . . . . . . . . . . . . . . . . . . .71
Mowll, Joshua    8-11   12-14 . . . . . . . . . . . . . . . . . . . . . .72, 117
Muchamore, Robert    12-14 . . . . . . . . . . . . . . . . . . . . . . . . . .117
Murphy, Jill    5-7   8-11 . . . . . . . . . . . . . . . . . . . . . . . . . . 23, 72
Nabb, Magdalen    5-7 . . . . . . . . . . . . . . . . . . . . . . . . . . . . . . . . 23
Naidoo, Beverley    12-14 . . . . . . . . . . . . . . . . . . . . . . . . . . . .118
Naifeh, Ted    12-14 . . . . . . . . . . . . . . . . . . . . . . . . . . . . . . . . .118
Napoli, Donna Jo    12-14 . . . . . . . . . . . . . . . . . . . . . . . . . . . .118
Nash, Margaret    5-7 . . . . . . . . . . . . . . . . . . . . . . . . . . . . . . . . 23
Nesbit, E    8-11 . . . . . . . . . . . . . . . . . . . . . . . . . . . . . . . . . . . . 72
Newbery, Linda    8-11   12-14 . . . . . . . . . . . . . . . . . . . . .72, 118
Nicholson, William    8-11   12-14 . . . . . . . . . . . . . . . . . . .72, 118
Nimmo, Jenny    5-7   8-11 . . . . . . . . . . . . . . . . . . . . . . . . . 24, 73
Nix, Garth    12-14 . . . . . . . . . . . . . . . . . . . . . . . . . . . . . . . . . .119
Norriss, Andrew    8-11 . . . . . . . . . . . . . . . . . . . . . . . . . . . . . . 73
Norton, Mary    8-11 . . . . . . . . . . . . . . . . . . . . . . . . . . . . . . . . 73
O'Brien, Robert C    8-11 . . . . . . . . . . . . . . . . . . . . . . . . . . . . . 73
O'Neill, Joan    12-14 . . . . . . . . . . . . . . . . . . . . . . . . . . . . . . . .119
Offen, Hilda    5-7 . . . . . . . . . . . . . . . . . . . . . . . . . . . . . . . . . . 24
Ogilvy, Ian    8-11 . . . . . . . . . . . . . . . . . . . . . . . . . . . . . . . . . . 73
Oldfield, Jenny    5-7   8-11 . . . . . . . . . . . . . . . . . . . . . . . . 24, 74
Oppel, Kenneth    8-11 . . . . . . . . . . . . . . . . . . . . . . . . . . . . . . 74
Oram, Hiawyn    5-7 . . . . . . . . . . . . . . . . . . . . . . . . . . . . . . . . 24
Paolini, Christopher    12-14 . . . . . . . . . . . . . . . . . . . . . . . . . .119
Parkinson, Siobhán    8-11 . . . . . . . . . . . . . . . . . . . . . . . . . . . 74
Patterson, James    12-14 . . . . . . . . . . . . . . . . . . . . . . . . . . . .119
Paver, Michelle    8-11   12-14 . . . . . . . . . . . . . . . . . . . . .74, 119
Payne, Tony and Jan    5-7 . . . . . . . . . . . . . . . . . . . . . . . . . . . 24
Pearce, Philippa    8-11 . . . . . . . . . . . . . . . . . . . . . . . . . . . . . . 74
Peet, Mal    12-14 . . . . . . . . . . . . . . . . . . . . . . . . . . . . . . . . . .120
Pennac, Daniel    8-11 . . . . . . . . . . . . . . . . . . . . . . . . . . . . . . . 75
Pennington, Kate    12-14 . . . . . . . . . . . . . . . . . . . . . . . . . . . .120
Peyton, K M    12-14 . . . . . . . . . . . . . . . . . . . . . . . . . . . . . . . .120
Pielichaty, Helena    8-11   12-14 . . . . . . . . . . . . . . . . . . 75, 120
Pierce, Tamora    12-14 . . . . . . . . . . . . . . . . . . . . . . . . . . . . . .120
Pilkey, Dav    5-7   8-11 . . . . . . . . . . . . . . . . . . . . . . . . . . 25, 75
Pirotta, Saviour    5-7 . . . . . . . . . . . . . . . . . . . . . . . . . . . . . . . 25
Plaisted, Caroline    8-11   12-14 . . . . . . . . . . . . . . . . . . .75, 121
Platt, Richard    8-11 . . . . . . . . . . . . . . . . . . . . . . . . . . . . . . . . 75
Postgate, Daniel    5-7 . . . . . . . . . . . . . . . . . . . . . . . . . . . . . . . 25
Potter, Beatrix    5-7 . . . . . . . . . . . . . . . . . . . . . . . . . . . . . . . . 25
Potts, Ghillian    5-7 . . . . . . . . . . . . . . . . . . . . . . . . . . . . . . . . 25
Potts, Stephen    8-11 . . . . . . . . . . . . . . . . . . . . . . . . . . . . . . . 76
Pow, Tom    12-14 . . . . . . . . . . . . . . . . . . . . . . . . . . . . . . . . .121
Powell, Jillian    5-7 . . . . . . . . . . . . . . . . . . . . . . . . . . . . . . . . 25
Powling, Chris    5-7   8-11 . . . . . . . . . . . . . . . . . . . . . . . . 26, 76
Pratchett, Terry    8-11   12-14 . . . . . . . . . . . . . . . . . . . .76, 121
Price, Susan    8-11   12-14 . . . . . . . . . . . . . . . . . . . . . . .76, 121
Priestley, Chris    8-11 . . . . . . . . . . . . . . . . . . . . . . . . . . . . . . 76
Prince, Alison    12-14 . . . . . . . . . . . . . . . . . . . . . . . . . . . . . . .121

Index

Prince, Maggie   12-14 ................................ 122
Pringle, Eric   8-11 ................................. 77
Prior, Natalie Jane   8-11 ........................... 77
Prøysen, Alf   5-7   8-11 ......................... 26, 77
Prue, Sally   12-14 .................................. 122
Pullman, Philip   8-11   12-14 .................. 77, 122
Rabb, M E   12-14 ................................... 122
Rai, Bali   8-11   12-14 ......................... 77, 122
Ransome, Arthur   8-11 .............................. 78
Rayban, Chloë   12-14 ............................... 123
Rayner, Shoo   5-7   8-11 ........................ 26, 78
Read, Anthony   8-11 ................................ 78
Rees, Celia   8-11   12-14 ....................... 78, 123
Rees, Gwyneth   5-7   8-11 ....................... 26, 78
Reeve, Philip   8-11   12-14 ..................... 79, 123
Rennison, Louise   12-14 ............................ 123
Richards, Justin   8-11 .............................. 79
Richardson, E E   12-14 ............................. 123
Riddell, Chris   5-7 ................................. 26
Ridley, Philip   8-11 ................................. 79
Riordan, James   12-14 .............................. 124
Riordan, Rick   8-11 ................................. 79
Rix, Jamie   8-11 .................................... 79
Roberts, David   8-11 ................................ 80
Roberts, Katherine   8-11   12-14 ............... 80, 124
Robinson, Catherine   12-14 ........................ 124
Robinson, Hilary   5-7 ............................... 27
Rodda, Emily   8-11 .................................. 80
Rodgers, Frank   5-7 ................................. 27
Rook, Sebastian   8-11 ............................... 80
Rose, Malcolm   12-14 .............................. 124
Rosoff, Meg   12-14 ................................. 124
Rowling, J K   8-11   12-14 ...................... 80, 125
Rusbridger, Alan   5-7 ............................... 27
Rushton, Rosie   12-14 .............................. 125
Ryan, Chris   12-14 ................................. 125
Ryan, Margaret   5-7   8-11 ..................... 27, 81
Sachar, Louis   5-7   8-11   12-14 .......... 28, 81, 125
Sage, Angie   5-7   8-11 ......................... 28, 81
Said, S F   8-11 ..................................... 81
Saunders, Kate   8-11 ................................ 81
Sedgwick, Marcus   12-14 ........................... 126
Serraillier, Ian   8-11 ............................... 82
Seuss, Dr   5-7 ...................................... 28
Sewell, Anna   8-11 .................................. 82
Shadow, Nick   8-11   12-14 ..................... 82, 126
Shan, Darren   12-14 ............................... 126
Sharratt, Nick   5-7 ................................. 28
Shearer, Alex   12-14 ............................... 126
Sheldon, Dyan   5-7   8-11   12-14 ........ 28, 82, 126
Shipton, Paul   8-11 ................................. 82